PSYCHOLOGY OF STORYTELLING

ARVIND UPADHYAY

What about you? Are you confused as to why God is leading you down a certain path? You know His voice is calling you, but you are unsure of your abilities. I can help you if your path involves speaking in front of people or oneon-one communication. I have been there, I know how you feel, and I can lead you through the exciting adventure God has for you. This book is for you! If I can speak before groups, you can too. You have no excuses, because I have already claimed them all. They belong to me. Since I own them, I can show you how to overcome them. In this book I will teach you some of the things God has taught me. He has made me qualified to help several types of people. First, I can help the inexperienced speakers. That's because I know where I came from. I started off with no speaking advantages. I have had to develop these skills by yielding to God's leading. Second, I have been amazed with the number of great speakers who have used this book to fine-tune their established communication skills. They tell me speaking was intuitive for them and they didn't have to work at it. Therefore they missed some of the basic steps. Learning those steps has made them even better communicators. This book is also for the person who never speaks in front of crowds, but deals with people one-on-one. This would include counselors, parents, grandparents, businesspeople, medical professionals, and others. "I COULD NEVER DO THAT" If you cringe at the thought of speaking in front of a crowd, I'm surprised you started reading this chapter. You remind me of Loretta. She couldn't believe she had let herself be talked into going to one of my storytelling workshops. For years her pastor had tried to get her to teach a Sunday school class. She was willing to help with food preparation and art projects, but she would never consent to teaching a class. Suddenly she found herself in a storytelling workshop.a group of ambitious entrepreneurs share their terrain with its year-round inhabitants: flamingos, a red-footed tortoise, and 35 Madagascar lemurs. "There are only 200 lemurs left in the world," Sir Richard Branson explains as a lemur attempts to jump from one tree to another. "And if he doesn't make it, they'll only be 199," Branson jokes. While the rare species of animals are a gift to behold, the entrepreneurs are hoping for a financial gift from Branson, the island's owner. The Virgin Group founder owns all 74 acres of this lush, tropical paradise called Necker Island. It's his home and his hideaway. On this day it's also the setting for the Extreme Tech Challenge, one of the most unusual pitch competitions the world has ever seen. The finalists—some of whom I coached to tell their product story more effectively—are here to sell Richard Branson on their ideas. Bill Tai, a career venture capitalist and a sponsor of the pitch competition, has been investing in companies since 1991. Tai has seen several waves of technology in Silicon Valley and he believes that now, more than ever, the ability to communicate ideas simply and clearly and to tell compelling stories is critical to standing apart in the marketplace of ideas. Technologists and scientists no longer talk to just their peers. If they can't explain the benefits of their products to consumers, their ideas won't catch on. They must translate the language of bits and bytes into a story every consumer understands. Tai has found a kindred spirit in Richard Branson, who strongly believes in the art of storytelling to drive change. "Telling a story is one of the best ways we have of coming up with new ideas, and also of learning about each other and the world," 1 Branson says. Branson intuitively knows what neuroscientists are confirming in the lab—our brains are wired for story. In order to understand Branson's belief that storytelling can make a positive impact in the future, we must look to the past. One million years ago humans gained control of an element that was critical to the survival of our species. The element helps explain why some pitches fail miserably while others succeed at launching a brand. It explains why many ideas fail to gain traction, while others trigger global movements. It explains why many leaders fail to inspire their teams, while others persuade people to walk through walls. The element is fire.

Anthropologists point to fire as the spark that ignited human evolution. It makes sense because once our ancestors got control of fire they could cook food, which radically increased the size of human brains. Fire also warded off predators at night, another positive if you wanted to live to see the sun rise. Until recently, however, few scientists studied one of the most profound benefits of fire— sparking our imagination through storytelling. Firelight extended the day, providing more time for purposes other than hunting and gathering. As people shared their personal experiences around the fire, they learned to avoid danger, to hunt more effectively as a team, and to strengthen cultural traditions. Social anthropologists believe storytelling made up 80 percent of the fireside conversations of our ancient ancestors. In Namibia's Kalahari desert, a group of nomads known as the Bushmen still spend their days foraging for food such as melons, nuts, seeds, and antelope. They are hunter-gatherers by day and storytellers at night. When the sun sets on the Kalahari, the Bushmen light fires and tell stories just as their ancestors did thousands of years earlier. During the day the Bushmen's conversations are focused on survival: hunting strategies, resource management, mediating disputes, etc. Only 6 percent of their conversations involve stories. 2 By night it's a different story, literally. As the embers of the fire extend the day, the Bushmen devote 81 percent of their conversations around the campfire to telling stories. Men and women tell stories, mostly about people the other villagers know and humorous or exciting adventures. For the Bushmen storytelling triggers the imagination, creates bonds between groups of people who don't know each other, and conveys information about institutions that are critical to the Bushmen's survival. Not all communicators have the skill of storytelling, even in tribal societies. Among the Bushmen, as among TED speakers or business leaders, the best speakers leave the audience rolling with laughter, still with suspense, or inspired to seek their own adventures. Camp leaders were often good storytellers. And the best of the best—the most admired storytellers—use "multimodal communication" such as gestures, imitations, sound effects, and songs. The Kalahari storytellers learned that they had to deliver information, convey experiences, inspire, and entertain. If people aren't entertained, they stop listening and go to sleep, not unlike what happens in millions of business presentations given every day. Humans evolved to perceive stories as entertaining because if they didn't pay attention, they might be a lion's lunch. "Stories told by firelight put listeners on the same emotional wavelength, elicited understanding, trust, and sympathy, and built positive reputations for qualities like humor, congeniality, and innovation," 3 says University of Utah anthropology professor Polly Wiessner. "Through stories and discussions people collected experiences of others and accumulated knowledge of options that others had tried. Night talk was critical for transmitting the big picture." Wiessner, who spent three months living with the Kalahari in northwest Botswana and recording their conversations, says that "appetites" for fire-lit settings remain with us to this day. The public's appetite for story is what makes some people very, very rich. More than 2,500 years ago a rhetorician named Gorgias learned that great storytellers can inspire audiences. He traveled around ancient Greece teaching rhetoric, specifically arguing that adding emotional stories in one's speeches can "stop fear and banish grief and create joy and nurture piety." Gorgias helped people craft stronger arguments, which won him many admirers. He became one of the wealthiest citizens of Greece on the strength of his storytelling. Telling great stories still makes people wealthy, especially entrepreneurs with an idea to sell.

Contents

1

The Tools Have Changed

———◦♡◦———

Back on Necker Island, Richard Branson has a smile on his face as he listens to entrepreneurs leverage the power of story to make him laugh, make him think, and inspire him to invest in their idea. The stories give Branson a new way of looking at the world and ultimately spark his imagination that world-changing innovations are not only possible in his lifetime, but that Branson himself can play a role in their development. Branson so loves storytelling around a campfire that he commissioned a local artist to build a beautiful hand-carved metal sphere to hold a giant fireball. The firelight talk might have started 400,000 years ago, but our brains are still wired for story today. Of course, the stakes have changed. Instead of hunting for food the entrepreneurs pitching Richard Branson are looking for cash. And the tools have changed, too. PowerPoint has replaced drawing pictures on a cave wall. But one thing hasn't changed, and it's our desire—a craving—to hear captivating stories. Those who have mastered the skill of storytelling can have an outsized influence over others. According to Princeton University neuroscientist Uri Hasson, a person who tells compelling stories can actually plant ideas, thoughts, and emotions into a listener's brain. The art of storytelling is your most powerful weapon in the war of ideas. On Necker, in the 10 minutes that each entrepreneur is given to articulate the vision behind their idea or product, they must grab Branson's attention, convince him that the idea has the potential to positively impact the world, and inspire him to make a substantial financial commitment to the company. Most people who are given 10 minutes to pitch their idea mistakenly assume that potential investors want to hear all about the financials, the numbers, and the data. They are only partly right. These entrepreneurs are neglecting the core findings of neuroscience: Emotion trumps logic. You cannot reach a person's head without first touching their heart and the path to the heart runs through the brain, starting with the amygdala.

The Amygdala: A Storyteller's Best Friend

For many years medical researchers believed that people could only get addicted to drugs and alcohol. Then, neuroimaging technologies emerged that allowed researchers to see blood flow in the brain revealing that humans are also addicted to activities like sex, gambling, food, and shopping. Some activities hijack the brain just as powerful drugs do. Drugs like heroin produce an especially powerful surge of dopamine—one so intense that a single hit can hook a person for life. Scientists are finding that the very same reward centers in the brain are also involved in persuasion, motivation, and memory. These findings have profound implications for your success. For example, researchers now know that a thought can elicit a "somatic state," meaning the thought triggers the same regions of the brain that would be activated if you were actually experiencing the event in real life. Let's say you win $20 million in a lottery. You'd be euphoric because your brain's amygdala —an almond-shaped mass of nuclei in your frontal lobe—would release a rush of the neurotransmitter dopamine, the pleasure chemical. Now close your eyes and imagine yourself winning the lottery. Picture the sights, sounds, and feelings around the event. Who's with you when you learn the news? What is their facial expression like? What are all of the things you can now do with the money? You might not realize it, but your mouth will gently curl up into a smile. You're getting a small shot of dopamine that's making you feel good because you are activating the same regions of your brain that would be triggered if you had actually won. That's the power of the amygdala. A great story releases a rush of chemicals like cortisol, oxytocin, and dopamine. Thanks to neuroscience we've learned more about storytelling in the last 10 years than we've known since humans began painting pictures on cave walls. We now know which brain chemicals make us pay attention to a speaker (cortisol) and which make us feel empathy toward another person (oxytocin). We also know what triggers those neurochemicals. We know what stories work, why they work, and we can prove it scientifically. Addiction to story isn't a bad thing. If inspiring storytellers didn't exist the world would be a far different place, and not for the better. For example, in a series of six speeches in 1940, British prime minister Winston Churchill succeeded in completely turning around public opinion in World War II. A nation that had resigned itself to appeasing Nazi Germany just 14 days earlier had decided to take up the sword and fight to the end after listening to Churchill's powerful argument. Although Germany had conquered large parts of Western Europe, Churchill masterfully painted a picture of the British successfully defeating Hitler's army. "What is our aim?" Churchill asked rhetorically. "Victory. Victory at all costs, victory in spite of all terror, victory, however long and hard the road may be; for without victory there is no survival." Through the storyteller's gift, Churchill radically altered the destiny of an entire civilization. Interestingly, Churchill wasn't born with the storyteller's gift. Like mastering any art, he had to work on it. Churchill had stage fright early in his political career. So did Richard Branson, and the famous pastor Joel Osteen. Billionaires Barbara Corcoran and Warren Buffett had a fear of public speaking, too. Great storytellers look effortless because they put a lot of effort into being great. History's most inspiring leaders were storytellers: Jesus, John F. Kennedy, Martin Luther King Jr., Ronald Reagan, Nelson Mandela, Henry Ford, and Steve Jobs. Many of today's most inspiring entrepreneurs and leaders are also storytellers: Richard Branson, Bill Gates, Mark Burnett, and Sheryl Sandberg. Many of the storytellers featured in this book changed the course of history. Some are business heroes. Some inspired movements. Above all, they are all dream makers. They reach for the stars and inspire the rest of us to create our own moonshots. This book is about the visionaries and risk-takers who have mastered the art of telling stories and who inspire us to live better lives. Some make us laugh. Some make us think. Some make us change. Through artfully telling stories that inform and challenge, they build companies, drive the world forward, and make us feel like we, too, can achieve the impossible. We're All Storytellers Storytelling is the fundamental building block of communication. In a world where people are bombarded by choices, the story is often the deciding factor in whom we decide to do business with. We're all storytellers. We tell stories to sell our ideas. We tell stories to persuade investors to back a product. We tell stories to educate students. We tell stories to motivate teams. We tell stories to convince donors to write a check. We tell stories to encourage our children to reach their full potential. Learn to tell a story and your life and the lives of those you touch will be radically transformed. The Storyteller's Secret features more than 50 storytellers who have changed the world or impacted business thanks in large part to mastering the art and science of storytelling. Each storyteller falls into one of five categories intended to inspire you to think differently about your own narrative, and how you can build storytelling into your everyday communication: · Storytellers Who Ignite Our Inner Fire · Storytellers Who Educate · Storytellers Who Simplify · Storytellers Who Motivate · Storytellers Who Launch Movements Each chapter is divided into three sections. First you'll learn about the storyteller's own story. Most of the men and women profiled in this book were at one time common people who used storytelling to achieve uncommon results. The second section of each chapter examines the storyteller's tools in more detail, why they work and how you can apply them. Finally, each chapter concludes with a short summary of the lesson learned—the storyteller's secret. Once you learn the storytellers' secrets and why they work, you can apply the techniques to almost any type of communication: public speaking, PowerPoint presentations, blogs, e-mail, advertising and marketing, or simply pitching an idea over coffee at Starbucks. You will learn to frame an idea to inform, illuminate, and inspire. In the next 10 years the ability to tell your story persuasively will be decisive —the single greatest skill—in helping you accomplish your dreams. Since the next decade marks the greatest promise civilization has ever known, the story you tell yourself and the story you share with others will unlock your potential and, quite possibly, change the world. Isn't it time you shared yours?

2

THE FOURTEEN STEPS

Step 1: Select a story Step 2: Push through the story Step 3: Envision the scene with present-day feelings and concerns Step 4: Tell the story from the view of someone at the scene Step 5: Establish the story's central truth Step 6: Find a memory hook Step 7: Tell a story within a story Step 8: Plan your first words Step 9: Know how the story ends Step 10: Research the facts Step 11: Eliminate needless detail Step 12: Add description to the story Step 13: Include audience participation Step 14: Arrange practice audiences

3

ADAPTING PRESENTATIONS FOR STORY THINKERS

Our culture has gone through a change that has altered our society. Many Christian ministries are becoming aware of it, but don't know how to respond. Other ministries have labeled it ungodly, so they ignore it and continue on as if nothing had changed. This cultural change is neither godly or ungodly. It is simply the difference in how people receive information and the way they remember information. People of past generations were considered analytical thinkers. For them, everything is linear. They think in facts and figures, and the best way to communicate to them is through an outline. If speakers want analytical thinkers to remember information for any length of time, they create points and put them in a creative order. For instance, they can have all the words of the outline start with the same letter. Better yet, the first letter of all the points can spell out a word. They don't feel the need to include a story, unless it reinforces the outline. Stories are props that illustrate the points, so they are no longer called stories. They are called illustrations. This was excellent preparation for past generations, but everything has now changed. Most people today receive information best if it is given to them in the form of stories. They are not linear thinkers but are what I call story thinkers. These people are some of the most creative, productive citizens of our society. They want the information, and they want it straight in a way that holds their interest. You still need a theme and even an outline; just don't let them know you have it. They don't want your clever tricks and ingenious alliterations. Stories are the best way to reach this new breed of thinker. TIME TO ADJUST I was invited to a school several years ago to teach creative writing to their students. The principal was concerned about my going into one particular fourth grade class. The teacher had tried everything but was frustrated. The principal told me, "The class is full of ADHD students. You are going to have problems there, so I better go with you in case you need my help." He sat in the back as I taught the class. He was amazed. I was using storytelling to teach the students to create, write, and rewrite. He watched as these students listened in rapt attention. He was astonished at how I kept the room in a constant state of chaos. Yet every student was learning and creating. They walked around the room, sat on the floor, talked to one another, participated in fun activities, and created fantastic compositions. This classroom was full of story-thinking students, and I was successful because I adjusted to their way of thinking. It may have seemed chaotic to an outsider, but it was organized and completely under my control. I teach adult Bible studies the same way, with the same results. People are encouraged to move around, talk to one another, express ideas, and be creative. No one knows exactly what to expect when they walk into class, but they know it is going to be fun and they will learn the Scriptures. Members of the class tell me they understand their Bible better and they are growing in their walk with God. We have taken this process into prisons and have watched it change lives. Inmates respond enthusiastically, and soon their entire worldview is changed. It is hard to maintain their reputation as a troublemaker when they are out in the yard telling Bible stories. Some wardens have told us it changes not only the prisoners but also the atmosphere of the entire prison. It is exciting when inmates learn this method and use it to teach the Bible to others. THE SCRIPTURES CONTAIN BOTH Jesus stood before Galileans and looked into their faces. He had a message and wanted them to listen and remember what He said. He told them stories. It is said Jesus was the master teacher because of His use of stories. No, He was the master teacher because He knew His audience and adapted His message to their way of thinking. Paul stood before Greeks and looked into their faces. He had a message and wanted them to listen and remember what he said. He used analytical reasoning to explain the gospel. He knew his audience and adapted his presentation. Later, when Paul went to Jerusalem, he neglected to adapt his presentation for the Jewish audience; instead he used the analytical method that worked so well with his Gentile audience. But the people standing before him were unmoved by his message.

Only the Romans listened to him. Don't make this mistake. Know your audience! Always present your message in a way that is consistent with how they think. The Bible reflects the different ways people receive and remember information. The various writers of Scripture wrote to either story thinkers or analytical thinkers. The Gospels are written in stories. To this day, they appeal to the story thinkers in our society. The Epistles are analytical and appeal to that type of thinker. Both need to be read and studied, but the appeal is different. STORYTELLING TECHNIQUES It is no longer acceptable to add an illustration near the end of a lesson, sermon, or business presentation. The techniques you will find in this book will give you the ability to skillfully adjust your message so you can talk the language of the people around you. Today your audience thinks in stories, they remember stories, and they will listen if you tell stories. A few years ago, a woman told me she was scheduled to speak to a particular organization, but was allowed only seven minutes to make her presentation. "How can I give my three important points and still have time to tell a story?" She was still thinking "linear" and wanted to add an illustration to her points. I showed her how to reverse that thinking. She was then able to create a seven-minute story that contained all three concepts she wanted to communicate. The key was to emphasize the story and not the points. I told her, "If you are brave enough to do this, your talk will be the most dramatic seven minutes of the day, and the audience will never forget it." ADAPTING YOUR PRESENTATION FOR MEN AND WOMEN Men and women generally receive information differently. Men tend to think in pictures, while women tend to think in words. I was in a meeting of businesspeople attended mostly by men. A woman came to talk about her business and how it related to our community. She spent the entire time telling us facts. She was giving us words not pictures. The men in the room might have stayed at the meeting out of courtesy, but every one of them left the room mentally. Each one was thinking about things unrelated to what she was talking about. I knew she had fantastic stories about her business that would have completely captivated this group, but she just wasn't using them. Since we were friends, I waited a few days and then made an appointment with her. I asked how she felt the meeting went. She knew it had not gone well but was puzzled as to why. I explained about the different thinking processes of men and women. I led her through a process where she put her points inside relevant stories. We worked on this together until we had created a presentation about herself, her clients, and the impact her business was making. It transformed how she has been received in the business community. She is able to tell all the facts, but they are hidden in interesting stories. Now her audiences pay attention to what she says. MAKING A PRESENTATION? · In one phrase, state what you hope to accomplish with your presentation. · Give three or four important aspects about the subject matter. · Craft several two-minute stories that illustrate each aspect. The number of stories is determined by the length of your presentation. · Weave these stories together to make a formal presentation. * Use the instruction in this book to increase how effectively you deliver this presentation. REACHING LISTENERS WITH STORIES People approach this book for different reasons. Some want to create stories designed to enhance business presentations or influence clients. Others specialize in children's stories for a Sunday school class or children's church. Perhaps you sense a need to put a new spark into family devotions and capture the hearts of your children. Pastors may be reading this book because they want to become more creative in the way they prepare and present sermons. Whatever the reason, we are all called to work with both analytical and story thinkers. We are to communicate to both men and women. As you keep reading, you will learn to prepare a story and present it in a way that leaves a lasting impression. You will increase the impact you will have on a wide variety of people, some you may not have been able to reach until now. EASY—HARD Connecting with story thinkers is easy compared to communicating with analytical thinkers. It will seem harder if you are already active in public speaking. That is because it is different from how you were trained. Look at it this way. Your training causes you to focus on a generation that is decreasing in numbers. As you read this book, practice each step, and do the exercises. It will show you how to communicate in a way your audience will hear and remember. Men and boys will listen with a higher level of attention. But more important, you will be able to reach out to a society that is desperate for your message. Oh, to make things simple, I am going to refer to you as "a storyteller." This doesn't mean I think you are a professional storyteller. It simply means you are one who plans to communicate to our "storythinking culture" through the use of stories.

4

Where Do You Find Your Stories

STEP 1: Select a Story Sometimes it is difficult to find a story that fits a particular occasion and also fits your personality. This is amazing since the world is full of stories. We have heard them all our lives, and some of them are our favorites. Still, when you need one, it's nowhere to be found. So I am going to simplify the "finding" process for you. Start with a few folktales. These have been classics down through the years. This may not be the type of stories you want to tell on a regular basis, but you can use them to help become a better storyteller. From there you can move into stories that better fit your purposes. The best way to find folktales is to talk to your local librarian. Call in advance and say you are developing your storytelling skills. Ask if they can help you find books that contain some old storytelling classics. They love to be asked for recommendations and will no doubt have a stack of books waiting for you when you arrive. PROCESS FOR CHANGING A STORY I was once asked to tell a story at our church's Thanksgiving service. My pastor wanted to add a little variety to this traditional service, and it was my job to help him do it. He had three requirements: The story was to be about twenty minutes long, it must have a Thanksgiving theme, and should contain a good Christian message. "Oh, by the way," he added, "try to make it enjoyable." I had to find a story that would be just right for this occasion. There is a world of possibilities that could be used. So what type of tale should I look for? Here are the criteria I use when I search for a story. LESS IS BETTER Start with a small story. It doesn't matter if you are to give a ten-minute presentation or forty-five-minute presentation. It is always best to start with a smaller story. The reasons are simple: • You want to practice adding description to the story, which will make it captivating. • You want to learn how to make the story relate to the specific needs of your listeners, which will make it relevant. So find a small story. This will give you room to develop it according to your personality and the needs of your listeners. The story will naturally expand to fill the time allotment. THE RESOURCE OF CHILDREN'S BOOKS Even though my Thanksgiving story was for an adult audience, I visited the children's department of my local library. Children's books are the best source for small, well-structured stories, while books written for adults are full of written description designed to entertain readers. This gets in the way of a storyteller. So I called my favorite children's librarian and said, "Georgianne, do you have any Thanksgiving stories?" Of course she did. She selected several she especially liked and put them aside for me. This saved me an enormous amount of work. If I had searched for a story by myself, I might have gone through a hundred books to find the one I wanted. A librarian is a storyteller's best friend. A QUALITY STORY Once I arrived at the library, I looked at the seven books Georgianne had selected. Now it was time to decide which story was the best for the occasion. Each person is different, so you will need to determine what is important to you. I look for two—and only two—qualities: Does the story resonate with me? I want my audience to see that I am excited about the story. I can't do this if I don't like it. Besides, once I have developed the story, I may end up telling it many times. It is important that I like the story. Do I like the ending? For me, a good ending is a nonnegotiable element. I can adapt the rest of the story to fit the occasion, but good endings are hard to find. Step nine will show you how to craft a good story ending, but it will save you a lot of work if the story already has a good one. It wasn't long before I found the story I could use for the Thanksgiving service. I crafted it using the fourteen steps in this book, and it turned out to be just what the pastor wanted. MAKING APPROPRIATE CHANGES I was asked to tell a cowboy story for a museum of history. I searched and searched, but I couldn't find one that resonated with me. Suddenly, I came across a Japanese story that had a great plot and a wonderful ending. By the time I had finished reworking it, the little family in the story no longer lived in Japan. They lived in western Wyoming in the late 1800s. Jim was trying to get his herd established, and his wife, Helen, was making a home out of a sod-roofed cabin. Their daughter was unaware she was isolated from civilization; instead, she made friends with local natives. Most important, she had a vivid imagination. The story fit the occasion and has delighted many audiences since. RED FLAG OF MEMORIZING While I am talking about selecting a story, I must wave a red flag about memorized stories. You will be tempted to think, I want to make sure I say everything just right. I don't want to leave anything out. These are legitimate concerns, but memorizing is not the solution. There are several disadvantages of memorized stories. Memorizing limits the number of stories you will tell. It is important for a storyteller to constantly develop new material. You may be able to commit a few stories to memory, but eventually you are going to reach your limit. Also, you will lose a memorized story if you don't continually review and rehearse it. You can learn only so many memorized stories before you run out of rehearsal time. Memorizing limits flexibility. A freestyle story is one that is not memorized and can be adapted for different audiences. These changes may come in the middle of a presentation. Sometimes a storyteller realizes a particular story is not going well. With a freestyle story, he can make quick adjustments, or simply rush to the ending. Flexibility is more valuable than the false security you might feel by memorizing the story. Memorizing doesn't protect you. There may be some good reasons to memorize a story, but security is not one of them. And yes, it is true that freestyle storytelling may occasionally have a few drawbacks. There will be times when you leave something out that should have been said. At other times, you will say the wrong words. I once told a story in which I had the main character guiding his boat with an "udder" rather than a "rudder." Still, forgetting things in a freestyle story will usually go unnoticed. The story will stand on its own without those statements you thought were so important. But with a memorized story, everything usually stops when you go blank and forget your lines. And believe me, no matter how well you have a story memorized, you will forget your lines at one time or another. I have memorized two story-poems, which I use to warm up my voice. I have quoted them for years and have rehearsed them on a regular basis. No one on this planet knows the lines better than I do. Still, on occasion, I forget the words in the middle of a performance. Memorizing may distract from ministry. The ultimate goal of those in any Christian ministry is to focus on people and their needs. The focus of a storyteller should be on the message and the response of the audience. Memorizing a story often turns the focus toward words—making sure they are correct. The performance often becomes story-centered rather than audience-centered. Memorizing makes you less "copyable." You may have the skills to overcome all of these obstacles and be good at preparing and presenting memorized stories. This is a rare talent, and you should definitely use it. Just keep this thought in mind. Others are not challenged to copy you. Every time

I give one of my memorized story-poems, I hear, "I could never do that." But when I tell a freestyle story, people come up afterward and ask how they can improve their own skills. They want to learn more about storytelling. The principle is this: however you serve the Lord, make sure it encourages others to do the same. In other words, be "copyable." WHAT DID YOU HAVE FOR BREAKFAST? Are you able to tell someone what you had for breakfast this morning? Of course you are. You don't write it out on a sheet of paper and memorize it. No, you simply move your eyes off to the side for a moment and then tell what you had. Why did you move your eyes? That is your way of mentally "looking at your breakfast." Once you see it, you tell what you saw. You should tell a story in the same way—see it in your mind, and tell what you see. I know it is hard to imagine yourself telling a story without having every word planned out. You think you should at least have notes. Believe me, they are not necessary. In this course, you will learn to simply tell a story without security props. And you'll have fun doing it. Don't rush ahead and memorize something. Tell your stories the same way you tell what you had for breakfast. Let them flow naturally and they'll easily come to mind whenever you have opportunity to tell them. SELECT A STORY It is time to take step 1. From the following list, we will start by working through the first one together, "A Girl and Her Dreams." After you have gone through all the steps with this story, choose another story from the list and go through all the steps a second time. 1. A Girl and Her Dreams 2. Big Friend, Little Friend 3. Lonely Shepherd Boy 4. Donkey's Impressive Attire 5. Father, Son, and Donkey 1. A Girl and Her Dreams A girl was the only daughter of a dairy farmer. She was an attractive girl, but her family was poor so she had no money for pretty clothes. The young men of her town didn't recognize her beauty and rarely noticed her. One day her father told her, "Today you may sell a bucket of milk. Buy eggs with the money so you can hatch some chickens of your own. When they are grown, you can sell their eggs and buy beautiful clothes." The girl began to dream about her chickens. She figured out how many eggs she wanted to sell each day. She would spend the money on new clothes. She carefully put the bucket of milk on top of her head so she could easily carry it to the market. As she walked along, she imagined herself wearing her new clothes and all the attention she would get from the young men in town. She thought, I won't even look at them. I'll simply turn up my nose and ... As she put her nose into the air, the pail of milk fell off her head and spilled on the ground. She watched the milk disappear into the ground, along with all of her dreams. That is when she learned: Don't count your chickens before they hatch. 2. Big Friend, Little Friend A lion was napping one warm afternoon when suddenly a small creature ran over the top of his nose. With one swipe of his paw, he caught the little mouse. The lion roared, "How dare you walk across my nose! I'm going to eat you." "Oh, no!" cried the mouse. "Please have mercy on me. I will never do it again. If you let me go, someday I'll do a favor for you." The whole idea made the lion laugh. How could a little mouse do him a favor? Still, he decided to let her go. Some time later, the lion walked onto a net trap. The trap sprung and the net pulled him up into the air, halfway between the earth and the tree branch above. There was nothing he could do. He was caught, and soon the hunters would be back to get him. The great lion roared, but the other creatures ran away. The little mouse recognized the voice of the one who had shown her kindness. She ran to the tree and saw the lion's desperate situation. She climbed up the tree and made her way down to the net. She nibbled as fast as she could, and chewed through the strands of the net. Soon it came unraveled, allowing the lion to escape. The lion learned that ... Sometimes my littlest friends are my greatest friends. 3. Lonely Shepherd Boy A shepherd boy was tending his sheep in the meadow. It was a lonely job, so he thought of a way he could have some fun. He rushed toward the village yelling, "Wolf! Wolf!" Several men from the village grabbed their weapons and ran to help him. They stayed with him for a while, but finally returned to the village when no wolf appeared. A few days later, the shepherd boy once again felt lonely, so he played the same trick. Again the villagers ran to help him. When no wolf appeared this time, the men knew they had been fooled. They were not happy about it. The next week, a wolf came out of the forest and began circling the flock of sheep. The boy yelled, "Wolf! Wolf!" But nobody came to help him. Because of this, the wolf killed several sheep from the boy's flock. When the boy complained to the villagers, one of the wise old men told him, "A liar will not be believed, even when he speaks the truth." 4. Donkey's Impressive Coat A small donkey was tired of his lowly life of serving others. He wondered what it would feel like to be "king of the beasts." One day he saw a large lion's skin lying out to dry. He suddenly got an idea. He worked his way into the lion's skin, which covered him quite well. Then he strutted through the forest. Other animals ran away in fear when they saw him. He realized his elegant coat gave him a new respect among the creatures. Suddenly the little donkey saw his master walking down the path. At first the man didn't recognize him, but thought he was a lion. The donkey was so proud of himself, he couldn't contain his joy any longer. He burst out with a loud "hee-haw." Immediately his master turned and walked up to the donkey. He pulled the lion's skin off the animal, put a rope around his neck, and led him back to the barn. There the donkey stood with his head down, waiting for his next chore. He finally said to himself, There is value in keeping your mouth shut. 5. Father, Son, and Donkey A farmer and his son were taking their donkey into town to sell him. As they walked along, they passed a neighbor lady. "What a waste," she said. "One of you ought to ride on the donkey." The farmer stopped and placed his son on the donkey's back. Next they walked past an old man working in his garden. "How shameful," he said. "Doesn't your boy have any respect for his elders?" Immediately the boy got off the donkey and his father got on. They passed two schoolteachers. One said to the other one, "Look how mean that father is to his son. He is riding the donkey and makes the boy walk." The father reached down and lifted up the boy, setting him in front. The donkey walked much slower now, carrying his heavy load. They passed the blacksmith at the edge of town. He paused from his work, looked up, and scolded, "How cruel of you to overwork your donkey this way. The two of you are strong enough to carry him." Awkward as it was, the father and his son managed to pick up the donkey and carry him through the town. They came to the man who was to buy the donkey. He laughed. "I'm not going to buy a donkey that can't even walk to market." As they walked back home with the donkey, the father said to his son, You can't please all the people all the time.

5

What Makes Your Heart Sing?

People with passion can change the world for the better. —Steve Jobs As the sun was setting over the Hudson River on a brisk October day two men stood on the terrace of a luxury apartment overlooking New York's Central Park. One man, a rebellious 26-year-old, dressed in a mock turtleneck and blue jeans, stared at his running shoes for a long time without saying a word. Then, as quickly as a light switch moves from off to on, he turned to the man by his side —a successful corporate executive who was one month shy of his forty-fifth birthday—and delivered the words that would transform the careers of both men and change the business world forever. On the balcony of the San Remo apartment building in March 1983, Steve Jobs turned to John Sculley and challenged him with a simple but devastating question: "Do you want to sell sugar water for the rest of your life or do you want to come with me and change the world?" Sculley had just turned down Jobs's offer to run Apple, saying that he intended to remain in his position at PepsiCo. Jobs's question, however, forced him to do some serious soul-searching. "I just gulped because I knew I would wonder for the rest of my life what I would have missed," Sculley recalls of the question that landed like a "punch to the gut." The punch to the gut. The "wow moment." The "aha" moment. Whatever you choose to call it, radical transformation can happen in an instant. But an idea can only catch on if the person with the idea can persuade others to take action. Otherwise, ideas are simply neurons firing off in a person's brain. The greatest waste is an unfulfilled idea that fails to connect with audiences, not because it's a bad idea, but because it's not packaged in a way that moves people. This is a book about ideas that did capture our imagination and change the world. It's about dream makers, visionaries, and risk-takers who mastered the art of storytelling to bring those ideas to life. Steve Jobs was undeniably the greatest business storyteller of our time. On the apartment balcony back in 1983 Sculley had witnessed the famous Steve Jobs "reality distortion field," a phrase coined to describe Jobs's mix of charisma and his ability to convince people that they could accomplish the impossible. Upon hearing the news of Jobs's passing in October 2011, Sculley said, "Steve Jobs was intensely passionate at making an important difference in the lives of his fellow humans while he was on this planet. He never was into money or measured his life through owning stuff…. A world leader is dead, but the lessons his leadership taught us live on." 1 Jobs's lessons do live on in the careers of former colleagues such as Apple chief designer Jony Ive, Apple CEO Tim Cook, Nest Labs founder Tony Fadell, or Disney's chief of animation John Lasseter. Jobs inspired them to communicate differently, to sell their ideas in a way that captured the public's imagination. Jobs revolutionized computer design, of course, but he was also a persuasive storyteller. Every public presentation that Steve Jobs gave resembled a Broadway play and had all the classic components of a great narrative: sets and surprises, heroes and villains. Nearly every major technology leader—and darn near every young entrepreneur—now tries to create "Steve Jobs–like" presentations. While anyone can copy the minimalist design of a Steve Jobs keynote presentation, it won't get them very far until and unless they learn the real secret to Steve Jobs's gift as a storyteller. And that gift wasn't on a slide. It was in his heart. The Storyteller's Tools The Storyteller's Tools In March 2011 the visionary who made "one more thing" a signature catchphrase took the stage one last time to reveal Apple's secret sauce. Steve Jobs, thin and weak from the cancer that would take his life a few months later, made an unexpected appearance to introduce a new product, the iPad 2. Few people in the audience expected Jobs to make an appearance because he was on his third medical leave. "We've been working on this product for a while and I didn't want to miss it," he told the cheering crowd. Jobs closed the presentation with this observation: It's technology married with liberal arts, married with the humanities, that yields us the result that makes our heart sing. In one sentence Steve Jobs captured the essence of what made him an inspiring storyteller. As it turns out Sculley had nailed it, too, when he said that Jobs was passionate about making a difference. Passion is everything and Jobs had plenty of it. Since he cofounded Apple in 1976 with his friend Steve Wozniak, Jobs combined passion, logic, and emotion to make a profoundly meaningful connection with his audiences. Jobs's ability to inspire a crowd is legendary. After interviewing Jobs's colleagues, presentation designers, and the people who knew him best for my book, The Presentation Secrets of Steve Jobs, I discovered that Jobs's secret to captivating an audience was not in the slide design, though the designs were beautiful. Many leaders now try to mimic Steve Jobs's presentation style (current Apple executives use the same design template for major product launches). Jobs captivated our imaginations because he had a wild and wondrous appreciation for how technology could change the world and he had the courage to express it. Your story begins with your passion. You cannot inspire unless you're inspired yourself. Passion is a puzzle. Most people know it when they see it, but they have a hard time discovering it for themselves. Steve Jobs discovered it by asking, "What makes my heart sing?" The answer to the question: What makes my heart sing? is a lot different than the answer to the question: What do I do? Steve Jobs made computers; building tools to help people unleash their creativity made his heart sing. The question of what makes one's heart sing goes to the core of Apple's DNA. Apple CEO Tim Cook repeats a version of the phrase in his keynotes and product launches. Cook once asked, "What do our hearts beat for?" On another occasion, the launch of a new iPad Air in October 2014, Cook was talking about the product's high customer satisfaction scores. "This is what makes our hearts sing," he said. Steve Jobs wore passion on this sleeve. In 1997 Steve Jobs returned to the company he had cofounded after being fired 12 years earlier. Jobs held a staff meeting where he talked about the role passion would play in revitalizing the brand. Marketing is about values. This is a very complicated world. It's a very noisy world and we're not going to get a chance to get people to remember much about us. No company is. And so we need to be really clear on what we want them to know about us. Our customers want to know who is Apple and what is it that we stand for. What we're about isn't making boxes for people to get their jobs done, although we do that well ... But Apple is about something more than that. Apple's core value is that we believe that people with passion can change the world for the better. 2 On June 12, 2005, Steve Jobs gave one of the greatest college commencement speeches in history. Jobs delivered the 2,250-word speech in 15 minutes. Steve Jobs, the storyteller, crafted the speech as a three-part narrative supporting one central theme: Do what you love. "Have the courage to follow your heart and intuition. They somehow already know what you truly want to become," Jobs told the graduates. The profoundly moving speech garnered well over 20 million views on YouTube. Apple employees say Steve Jobs's passion continues to live in Apple's DNA and they mean it, literally. When Apple released a new version of its operating system, OS X, they secretly hid a gift, knowing that someone would discover it. Embedded in the Mac's word processing application—Pages—is the entire text of Jobs's commencement speech. Passion is contagious. Passion is irresistible. Passion fuels the inner fire.

Ask Yourself, What Makes My Heart Sing? Your passion is not a passing interest or even a hobby, but something that is intensely meaningful and core to your identity. For example, I play golf as a hobby. While I like the game—love it, actually—it is not core to who I am. It is, however, core to international PGA golf superstar Rory McIlroy. Asked to describe his love for the game McIlroy once said, "It's what I think about when I get up in the morning. It's what I think about when I go to bed." For McIlroy, golf isn't just a passing interest; it's the verse that makes his heart sing. I was invited to deliver a keynote speech at the prestigious LeWeb conference in Paris, a gathering of the world's most passionate entrepreneurs for several days of sharing information on technology, innovation, and entrepreneurship. Backstage I met Ferran Adrià, the visionary chef who created the world's most famous restaurant, El Bulli. "What is the one quality that all successful entrepreneurs share?" I asked Adrià. "That's impossible to answer," he responded. "There are so many paths to success." Adrià turned away and I figured it signaled the end of our conversation. Adrià then turned to me and said, "I take it back. There is one thing that all successful entrepreneurs have in common, and that's passion." "How do you know it when you find it?" I asked. "Let's put it this way. When you see a glass of wine, what do you think of?" "A drink," I said. "Exactly. You see a beverage. I see a vineyard. I see an ingredient. I see joy. I see family. I see friends. I see celebration." I enjoy wine, but for Adrià it makes his heart sing in celebration. Several years ago I interviewed Chris Gardner, the man portrayed by actor Will Smith in the movie, The Pursuit of Happyness. Gardner recounted his story of being homeless, spending nights in the bathroom of a subway station along with his two-year-old son. In the daytime Gardner would put on his one suit, drop off his kid at day care and take unpaid classes to become a stockbroker. You can guess how the story ends. Gardner rose to the top of his firm and became a multimillionaire. When I worked in San Francisco, I would take the BART train and pass the very subway station where Gardner and his son slept at night. I would look around at the faces of the people seated near me. Very few seemed happy. They were staring at cell phones with frowns on their faces or looking out the windows with glazed expressions of longing. The spark in their eyes had gone out. Somewhere along the way they had lost sight of their passion. I wondered: How it is possible for a homeless guy sleeping in the subway bathroom to have more excitement for life than those who had a job and rode the subway to work? I asked Gardner that very question. His answer changed my life. Gardner said, "The secret to success is to find something you love to do so much, you can't wait for the sun to rise to do it all over again." 3 Gardner rose from the depths of poverty precisely because he listened to the verse that made his heart sing. If you have yet to find your passion, ask yourself a better question. Don't ask, What do I want to do? Ask yourself, What makes my heart sing? Both questions will lead to very different answers. Before you learn the craft of storytelling and master the specific techniques that will help you inspire the world with your ideas, you must get really clear on what you want people to know about you. Begin the process by asking yourself the right questions. For example, I met with the startup team behind a healthcare company that enjoyed the backing of some of Silicon Valley's largest venture capital firms. The company had developed a blood test to detect cancer. I asked the CEO a series of four questions intended to elicit an emotional response and lead to a message the company could use to tell its story to its key audiences (investors, medical professionals, and the media). Note how each question gets progressively more emotional and triggers a very different response: 1. Why did you start a company? "To impact patients' lives." 2. What does your company do? "We've developed a tool that allows us to fight cancer with a simple blood test." 3. What are you passionate about? "Patient care. Every week we see patients matched with therapies that can save their lives." 4. What makes your heart sing? "We were working with an oncologist who told us about a patient they had diagnosed with pancreatic cancer. It had spread everywhere. The patient was told she had two months to live. There was no hope. Her oncologist knew about our blood test and decided to give it a try. The test results had successfully found the mutation of the patient's cancer. The mutations were inconsistent with pancreatic cancer. The patient had ovarian cancer. Her oncologist changed the treatment. In twelve weeks she had no detectable cancer. These stories keep me burning the midnight oil and working through the night." Reflect on what had happened in the previous conversation. The first three questions elicited factual responses. The fourth question—what makes your heart sing—triggered a story. Facts alone don't inspire. The heart of your story gives facts their soul. Fact-filled PowerPoint presentations do not win hearts and minds; stories do. Well-designed slides complement the story, but the story must come first. Disney animation chief John Lasseter, who said he owes his career to Steve Jobs, once said that in developing a story, the plot can change dramatically: the characters can come and go, as can the setting. What you can't change is the heart of the story because it lays the foundation for everything else. A famed venture capitalist once told me that he listens to a pitch as he would a song. He asks himself, Will its verses click with consumers? Will its emotional hook inspire people to join the hero's journey? The investor is looking for an emotional connection. He's listening for a pulse, a passion. The first step to telling an inspiring story is to discover your verse, the track that makes your heart sing. The Storyteller's Secret Inspiring storytellers are inspired themselves. They are very clear on their motivation, on the passion that drives them, and they enthusiastically share that passion with their audiences. Ask yourself, What makes my heart sing? The answer is the foundation upon which all great stories are built.

6

Let Them walk in your shoes

---♡---

The flickering fireplace looked so inviting, displaying colorful hues of orange and yellow. I leaned back in my easy chair, listening to the crackle and hiss of burning wood and enjoying the faint scent of smoke. It added warmth to a cold winter evening and offered comfort at the end of a hectic day. I thought, A good story would be the perfect complement to this cozy setting. I was in the mood for one that came from the Old Testament, so I picked up the Bible and turned on the side lamp. The page fell open to 2 Kings 4. My eyes skimmed to verses 38–41, which in my Bible had the heading "Elisha heals the noxious pottage." I read the passage several times to make sure I understood what was recorded about this incident. I wondered if it were part of a greater series of events, so I read the few chapters that came before. They didn't add much light on what happened. The account stood by itself. Although I had no intention of telling this in front of an audience, I took the story to step 2 without a second thought. I wanted to gain a better understanding of what might have happened that day. In fact, I mentally walked through all three steps in this chapter. When I finished reading, I turned off the lamp and looked into the flickering fire, watching the story unfold before my eyes. The prophet Elisha and his small group of men were camped in a region called Gilgal, and several of them had gone out to gather provisions for a meal. I walked with a young man who found some gourds. He didn't know they were poisonous. Without mentioning it to anyone, he went back to the fire, took out his knife, and shredded them into the stew. I was there. It was convenient that my fire was a lot like theirs. The drama unfolded before me: the pot of stew on the open fire, the poison that contaminated the precious food, and the miracle of the servant of God. I enjoyed being in Gilgal that evening with the School of the Prophets. And what an honor it was to meet Elisha. It all happened because I was willing to have them "walk in my shoes." Now it is time for you to practice the next step. Let's take it together with the story "A Girl and Her Dreams." Later you can come back and apply it to the other story you selected. STEP 2: Push through the Story This step is simple but critical. Once you have read the story several times, put the book aside and talk through it. This is a good time for you to find your "designated listener." This is someone who agrees to hear all the new stories you will be learning. The job of a listener is to appear sincerely interested in your story as you go through the process of the telling. Jan is my designated listener. It is true you can merely tell your story to a chair or a lamp, but it is far better if you tell it to another person. Still, the important part is to talk completely through the story without looking at the written version. You are going to be tempted to "perform" the story, but don't jump ahead. At this point simply tell what you know about the story. Pushing through a story has several benefits: · It takes the story off the written page and puts it into a telling form. This is an informal telling of the story; so don't worry about getting all the details correct at this point. · It helps you see if you have all the important facts straight in your memory. While you don't need to remember all the details, the structure does need to be in place. · It gives you a chance to see if you enjoy telling this story. Simply reading it doesn't provide you this gauge. Sometimes I like reading a story, but it goes flat once I tell it. Other times a story will seem dull when I read it, but it comes alive when I tell it. Remember, storytelling is an art form best developed in front of people. Even though it is best to be alone when you practice other performing arts, this isn't true with storytelling. You need to enlist the help of others. Before we are done with all fourteen steps, you will have five designated listeners! PUT THE CLAY ON THE WHEEL I compare "pushing through the story" to putting clay onto the potter's wheel. Before the potter can create a sculptured piece of art, he must remove the clay from its bucket and put it onto the table or wheel. By pushing through a story, you are taking a written narrative out of the book (the potter's bucket), and putting it into your mind (the potter's wheel). The story is raw and undeveloped, but it has potential. To simply think about the story without telling it is like merely looking at the clay in the bucket. It doesn't get the job done. Take the story out of the bucket, push through it, and listen to yourself tell it. So let's get started: · Find a designated listener. · Read "A Girl and Her Dreams" two times. · Set the book aside and talk through the story with your listener. Make it simple. · After you have completed this step, read the story one more time. If you are doing this in a class, · Divide into groups of four. · Have each person select a different story from the list in chapter 2. · To practice this step, each group should subdivide into two sets of partners. · Read your selected story two times. · Set the book aside and talk through the story with your partner, making it simple. · After each of you have completed this step, read the story one more time. MOVE AWAY FROM THE BOOK Don't look back at the written story once you have pushed through it and reread it once. It is important to move away from the written format and begin shaping the spoken format. STEP 3: Envision the Scene with Present-Day Feelings and Concerns A story becomes good when we tailor it so it relates to people who feel, think, act, react, and talk like we do. Our stories will have the greatest influence on people who live near us and are a part of our culture. So let's look at our story. It is an Aesop's fable. It will come alive with your audience if you can craft it so it relates to the feelings and concerns of the girl. But somehow it needs to be applicable to what your listeners are going through. They want "feelings and concerns," not a lecture about dairy farming or a discussion about keeping chickens for egg production. The purpose of step 3 is to allow the characters in your story to walk in your shoes. They should think like you and feel what the members of your audience feel. In your story, they have the same concerns, heartaches, and frustrations that reign in your home, school, church, workplace, and group of friends. AT THE SCENE Here is an exercise that will help you accomplish step 3. I call it "At the Scene." If you do it alone, I recommend you sit back in a relaxed position. When I do it, I often dim the lights and lean back in my easy chair. Picture yourself standing at the farm. No one can see you, but you can see everything that is happening. In fact, you can feel what they are feeling, and you know what they are thinking. Answer each of the following questions. · Look around the farm and describe what you see. · What do the girl and her father look like? Describe each one. · Describe the sounds you hear. · What do you smell? · What is the weather like? · Describe the feelings, attitudes, and moods of the girl. · Describe the feelings, attitudes, and moods of the father. · What are they thinking at the different times of the story? · Describe some of the chores the girl had to do on the farm. · What types of animals are on this farm? · Describe the girl's mother. · Describe some of the girl's friends. · Describe the attitudes and feelings of the young men mentioned in the story. Most of the sights, sounds, smells, and descriptions that come to mind will never be mentioned when you tell the story. It is only important that you have a clear picture of the situation from your life perspective. GIVE IT A TRY: Once you have completed the "At the Scene" activity, tell "A Girl and Her Dreams" to your designated listener. Add in as many of the feelings and concerns as you can. What! You don't have a designated listener yet? Well okay, tell it aloud to a piece of furniture near you. But you need to find that listener soon. If you are doing this in a class, do this exercise with your partner after the "push through the story" step. · One of you asks the questions and the other answers with whatever comes to mind. · Once both of you have had a turn at answering the questions, redivide the "group of four" so everyone has a different partner. · Tell your selected story to your new partner—adding in as many of the feelings and concerns as you can. You probably have a tremendous story already, but be patient. It is not close to finished yet. STEP 4: Tell the Story from the View of Someone at the Scene Telling the story in the first person gives you a better understanding of the emotions involved within a story and allows you to experience them. By doing this, the emotions are no longer "at arm's length." It makes the story much more personal. So tell "A Girl and Her Dreams" as if you were the girl. Then tell it as if you were the father. Although I go through this exercise personally, rarely do I keep the first person perspective when I tell a story to an audience. Most of my stories are told from the narrator's viewpoint. Still, as I tell it, that first person has a way of speaking up every now and then. I tell the Lion and the Mouse story ("Big Friend, Little Friend" on your list). As the narrator I tell about the little mouse being caught on the lion's nose. Suddenly the lion starts talking, scolding the mouse and threatening her life. I go back to being the narrator, but the mouse wants to talk. She is devastated with fear and can hardly get the words out. By telling your stories as a narrator, you can slip into several emotional viewpoints with ease. If you stay with the first person, you are stuck with how only one character feels. Now it is your turn to try it. Tell the whole story from one viewpoint and then the other. Finally tell it as a narrator but let each character take turns talking. IF YOU ARE DOING THIS IN A CLASS, · Work with your second partner as a way of getting ready for telling the story in the first person. · Redivide the group of four so everyone has yet a different partner (their third). · Each person tells their selected story in the first person. · After this first person telling, discuss how each story could be told as the narrator, and yet keep all the emotions that were in the first person telling. · Redivide the group of four so everyone has their original partner. · Tell your story as the narrator. In this way, everyone can see how improved their partner's story has become.

ratemark# 7

Make It Unforgettable

She cleared her throat and struggled to find the right words. The question had caught Julie off guard. She, along with several others from the women's Bible study, had attended a retreat. Now they were sharing their experience with the group. Julie had no problem telling about the wonderful fellowship and the new friends she had made. Everyone laughed when she excitedly described the water balloon fight. She explained how the special music and workshops had blessed her. Suddenly the leader of the Bible study asked her if she had attended the workshop titled "Seven Easy Steps to Walking in the Spirit." "Why yes, I did," she said hesitantly. She didn't want to admit she had almost fallen asleep in that session. "Oh, good. I went to college with the presenter; she is such a wonderful person. Tell us a little about her session." Julie's mind raced to think of at least one thing the speaker had said. She finally dodged the question by enthusiastically telling about another workshop titled "Reflecting His Image." "It was wonderful. The speaker was a pastor's wife from Montana, and she told real-life experiences that had us laughing one minute and in tears the next." Before Julie was able to catch herself, she told the group about the entire workshop. She didn't answer the leader's question, but she did increase the ladies' interest in attending next year's retreat. Why did Julie remember one workshop in its entirety, yet couldn't recall one statement from the other? It's simple. The pastor's wife from Montana had applied all three of the following storytelling steps to her workshop. These are the little secrets that make a big difference when you want your sermon, story, presentation, or speech to be unforgettable. Why is this crucial? You may have only one opportunity to influence an individual, a group of people, or a business associate. Most of those who hear you speak will not respond to your content immediately, and you may never see some of them again. Therefore, you need to make a lasting impression. Later in their lives, they will come to a point when they are making an important decision. Your goal is for your story or presentation to return to their minds. Most people think the key to an unforgettable speech is good preparation and tremendous content. These are essential. But we all have heard business presentations, Bible lessons, and workshops that were well prepared and had tremendous content, yet we've forgotten what was said within an hour. The same is true with a story. STEP 5: Establish the Story's One Central Truth To make a story unforgettable, ask yourself, "What motivates me to tell this story?" This could be simple, such as wanting people to relax and laugh a little. Or it could be to communicate a deep, abiding truth. A story, in its purest form, doesn't overtly assert its central truth. Jesus often told a story without giving it a theme. Still, He definitely had a reason for telling it, so His stories were unforgettable. People have been studying them for centuries. In many cases, people won't grasp the central truth behind a story, even if you tell them what it is. That is not the point here. The focus of step 5 is not on the listener but on the one crafting the story. The central truth controls how the plot is prepared and inspires the person telling it. For a story to make a lasting impression upon listeners, the teller must have a definite reason for telling it. MAKE THE CENTRAL TRUTH POINTED Your central theme is best if it is specific. Don't choose a generic one such as, "Have faith in God," "Trust God at all times," or "Endure hardships." These three would be better stated if they were like this: · Faith can sometimes run contrary to your experience. · Learn to trust in God, even if you are confused about what He's doing. · Endurance will turn frustrations into faith. As I mentioned, the theme does not have to be life changing. I tell a simple story that I feel teaches "imagination can comfort you in hard times." I never say those words while I am telling the story, and I'm sure no one thinks of those words when I am finished. Still, the theme is there, and it influences the flow of the story. GIVE IT A TRY: Think of the truth behind "A Girl and Her Dreams." Being an Aesop's fable, a central truth is stated at the end. For the sake of this exercise, think of a different central truth. You will be amazed how it changes your telling of the story. Here is a list of questions to ask yourself. Your answer to these questions becomes the theme of your story. · Why would I take the time to tell this story? · Why is it important? · What one truth do I want to communicate to my listeners? Once you choose a new central truth for "A Girl and Her Dreams" write it out so it becomes clear in your mind. Now tell the story with that truth in mind. STEP 6: Find a Memory Hook A memory hook is a phrase, song, concept, or attitude repeated throughout the story. It is not the theme but simply a memory booster. Don't be discouraged if you find this challenging, since developing a memory hook may be the hardest step in the process. For now it is important that you know about the principle. Once you know about it, you will see others using it. In time you'll be able to incorporate it into your own stories. Once you have mastered it, you will find this a great tool for making a lasting impression on people. SUBTLE OR BLATANT In some stories, the hook is subtle. In others, it is prominent or blatant. I repeat the subtle hook when I tell a story called "Gentile Dog." The audience doesn't realize I am repeating the phrase "us and them." I give it several times as a statement, once as an illustration, and finally I allow characters to act it out. I use the subtle approach with this story because I feel it would distract from the impact of the plot if I make the repetition too obvious. Still, I want the theme to go into the memory of my audience, so I cloak the hook to make it gentler. I tell a traditional folktale entitled "Dry Fry." In it, I repeat the phrase, "because around here, everybody knows Dry Fry!" It is so deliberate that after the first two times, the audience is repeating it with me. The best example of a memory hook is one used by Martin Luther King Jr. Many of us can still hear his inflections and emphasis as he repeated the phrase "I have a dream." His repetition of this memory hook helped make his presentation memorable for years. In a thirty-minute story about Joseph, I openly repeat the phrase "Remember Joseph!" When I tell the story of Jonah, I repeat "It's not fair!" over and over. Another illustration of a memory hook in a sermon is "It's Friday, but Sunday's coming!" by Tony Campolo. Once you hear it, you will never forget the hook, which helps you remember the sermon and its theme. A HOOK FOR ADULTS I have seen pastors keep children spellbound as they use a memory hook in children's church. Unfortunately, the tool is often missing when they speak to their adult audiences. Memory hooks are effective with adults as well as children. A blatant hook makes a story unforgettable. I can return to a church several years after telling one of these stories, and people will come and tell me they remember the key phrase. Each time you repeat a memory hook in a story, it must be with a straight face as if it were the first time. It is sometimes best to slow down when saying it. If you want people to repeat it with you, make sure you pause before saying it. Even a slight hand gesture invites people to join in. A good memory hook needs to fit the story. It is not enough to simply repeat a phrase. It should do one of the following: · Relate to a quality trait of the main character · Reinforce the underlying plot · Emphasize the theme A HOOK FOR CHILDREN When telling a story to small children, I usually use a singing memory hook. I'm sure those jingles have annoyed parents for days after story time. These are not musical masterpieces but simple, repeating phrases put to music. I said step 6 was a hard one. Don't worry about it if you can't think of a memory hook for your story. Still, give it a try. You might surprise yourself. STEP 7: Tell a Story within a Story

A couple of years ago I found myself in the presence of a master storyteller who wove a tale about his boyhood. He told about his childhood town and the unique people who lived there. His story centered on an older couple who owned a one-room grocery store, and into this setting, he wove at least three different story lines. "What impressed me the most," the storyteller remembered aloud, "was a small photo they kept on the counter. It proudly boasted the images of their seven grandchildren. The photo was positioned so that anyone who came into the store would see it, which encouraged comments about how beautiful the children were." (Without hesitating, the storyteller smoothly delved into a second story.) It seems that one of those children was Andrew who grew up and went off to Tahiti. During his expedition, he met a lady who was an American, but had lived on the island since she was born. They eventually fell in love and were married. When the store owners attended the wedding, they were amazed to find that the bride's father was an old high school friend! He had moved to Tahiti twenty-five years before. (This started a third story the storyteller skillfully integrated into the other two.) Even with two stories being added to the original one, it flowed so easily we didn't realize what he was doing. It all seemed so natural. In the end, all three stories smoothly closed at about the same time. Generally, telling a story within a story is a more advanced storytelling technique. Yet, if you learn to use this tool, it will increase your ability to use storytelling as a ministry tool. PROCEED WITH CAUTION Most stories don't need step 7, and often it would be awkward if you used it. Still, there comes a time when this ability is useful. To do this: · There must be a relationship between the stories. · Both stories must relate to the theme. · One story should illustrate a point within the other story. POSSIBLE USES To layer stories in this way, I have used short fables, old television advertisements, personal experiences, childhood memories, Bible illustrations, object lessons, audience involvement, songs, and short folktales. The options are endless. GIVE IT A TRY: Think of a side story you could tell inside "A Girl and Her Dreams." Possibly something that happened in the girl's school. Maybe tell how her parents first started in the dairy business. Perhaps you could tell about ... Oh, I'll let you think of something.

8
Know your ramble

When I say rambling, I am referring to a style of storytelling that is not memorized so it can easily conform to the audience. A story needs to be flexible. It will change if it is told to teenagers in a youth group, senior citizens in a retirement home, children in a library, or adults in a parent/ teacher meeting and so on. The storyteller can modify a rambling, freestyle story to meet the needs of an audience and still keep the story within a designated time frame. However, there are two parts of a story where the storyteller should not ramble: the first few sentences and the last few sentences. These should occupy a huge amount of your preparation time. Once you have crafted those beginning and ending sentences, memorize them! Know exactly what your first and last words will be before you stand in front of an audience. A FEW SECONDS OF ATTENTION A phenomenon happens when you step in front of a group of listeners, something few speakers recognize and use to their advantage. When you step up, you have the undivided attention of your audience ... for a few seconds. This is because you are the most active thing in the room. Let me emphasize this. You have their full attention for a few seconds, and no more. In that length of time, the audience will subconsciously make a snap judgment about how pleased they are that you are standing in front of them. If you don't seize this moment, their minds will conclude they have more important things to think about. Oh, you can regain their attention, but it is not easy. It is far better to seize it while it is being offered and not let it go. In those beginning seconds, know exactly what you are going to say ... and say it. This is where you will begin polishing your story for maximum audience impact. Carefully crafted "first and last words" become a frame for your story. So write them out, memorize them, and practice giving them until they are smooth and natural. Let's start with the first few lines of your story. STEP 8: Plan Your First Words As soon as Martha was introduced, she stepped on the platform and said, "I'm so glad to be here today. I have looked forward to coming for such a long time. As Bev said, my name is Martha, and I am excited about the story that I am going to tell you. I first heard it from my grandpa who …" [a few minutes of useless information about her grandfather]. "Well, let's see. It's time to tell the story. Many years ago there lived … Oh, wait, you need to know that this takes place in Bulgaria. Anyway, many years ago …" This is not the way to start a story, or any presentation. You need to know exactly what you are going to say when you first open your mouth. Don't leave it to chance. This is not the time to "wing it." You can ramble later. Generally speaking, here are some things not to say. · The name of my story is … · Once upon a time … · I heard this story years ago when … · I'm so glad to be with you today … · I'm not a very good storyteller, but … · Now, boys and girls, this story … Here are a few examples of how I start some of my favorite stories. · Buddy was top dog. When he walked down the street, all the other dogs just moved out of the way. · Hiram was a proper Jewish man. He was not one to rush into anything. · Jesus took a vacation. Did you know that? · There was a time when I would have made sure you knew who I was. · She climbed to the upstairs of her house. At the end of the hall, she sat next to the window. She groaned inside as she looked over the wall behind her house. Several skills are common among good storytellers. One is the ability to pull the audience into the heart of the story within the first few sentences. I will give you two principles to help you develop the skill of crafting great beginnings: "Get to the mountain" and "Find the entry door." 1. Get to the mountain. In one of my workshops, I told everyone to tell a story to a partner. There was an uneven number, so I stepped in and had a woman tell me her story. She was telling about a trip they took in India. Soon I looked at my watch and said it was time for me to stop the exercise for the class. She said, "Oh … uh … I haven't told my story yet." I was confused. I said, "What have you been telling me all this time?" "That was the introduction. The story is about our crazy taxi ride up the mountain. I was just explaining how we got to the mountain." She allowed me to use this as an illustration for the class. I told them, "Don't spend a lot of time introducing the story. Quickly get to the mountain!" That is what we want to hear. It is acceptable to tell a story without people knowing all the details of what led up to it. There are some situations where you need to introduce yourself or make some formal comments. But when it is time for your presentation, let the story make its own introduction. Get to the mountain so we can enjoy hearing about that crazy taxi ride. Here's another example of "getting to the mountain." I joined the choir when I was new to our church. The director did a masterful job of organizing the Christmas cantata that first year. His skill in presentation was superb. The audience was moved by the message they heard in the music. When we had sung the last note and the orchestra's last chord had faded, Pastor Wingate rose and moved up the steps toward the pulpit. I thought, Oh no, he is going to ruin it. Many pastors don't plan their first words after a moving presentation of the gospel in song. Usually they say, "My, what a wonderful cantata. Thank you, choir, for an excellent job. Let's give them a big round of applause. Now take out your Bibles, and turn to the book of Romans." The audience members inwardly groan, and their minds leave through the back door. I watched as Pastor Wingate walked toward the pulpit. The sound crew activated his lapel mic. Halfway across the platform, he started talking. His first words formed the beginning of a story. Instantly, the congregation was captivated. Everything that needed to be said went into his story and he skillfully included the Scripture. With ease he brought it to a conclusion and gave an invitation to answer God's call. I stood in awe. I had never seen the conclusion of a powerful cantata handled so brilliantly. The focus of the evening never left the message because our pastor had thought carefully about how he was going to start his remarks. 2. Find the entry door. Now comes the decision. Which is the best entry door for getting into the story? the beginning? the middle? the end? Remember, you want to quickly pull the audience into your presentation. Sometimes the beginning is not an exciting place to enter into the story. Look everything over and find a more interesting spot. Once you find it, start the story and then flash back to the beginning. I'll use "A Girl and Her Dreams" to illustrate. Here is the beginning: "A girl was the only daughter of a dairy farmer. She was an attractive girl, but her family was poor so she had no money for pretty clothes." Here is the middle: "The girl began to dream about her chickens. She figured out how many eggs she wanted to sell each day. She would spend the money on new clothes." Here is the end: "The pail of milk fell off her head and spilled on the ground. She watched the milk disappear into the ground, along with all of her dreams." · Starting at the beginning might sound like this: "Helen was an attractive girl, but no one knew it. She lived on a dairy farm and her family was poor ..." · Starting in the middle might sound like this: "This had to be the best day of Helen's life! She was going to raise chickens! This may not sound exciting to you, but for Helen it was life changing. You see, she was the only daughter of a dairy farmer …" • Starting at the end might sound like this: "Helen stood there in shock as she watched milk soaking into the ground. 'Oh,' she thought. 'This is the worst day of my life!' It all started that morning when her father told her exciting news …" It's true that most people enter the story at the beginning. It can usually be crafted in a way that draws the audience into the life of the story. The key is, find the best way to do this. Start there, and then go back to the beginning. GIVE IT A TRY: You have developed your sample story to a point where you can now add the polish of well-crafted "first words." (1) How can you quickly get into the story? (2) Where is the best place to enter into the story? Write the exact words you want to say when you begin "A Girl and Her Dreams." STEP 9: Know How Your Story Ends Susan was telling a wonderful story when she realized she didn't know how to end it. In an attempt to solve this problem, she just kept talking, hoping the perfect conclusion would suddenly present itself. When it didn't, she finally stumbled to an awkward ending and the story crashed. This ruined the effect that she had created for her listeners. Crafting a good story ending is difficult. Like I said earlier, try to find a story that already has a good ending. It will save you a lot of time. Still, here are some ideas on creating your own. 1. Finding the story ending People tend to worry more about the middle of the story and think the ending will take care of itself. It won't! Plan it out ahead of time. It is the focus of the entire story. The following are some ways not to end a story. There are always exceptions, but try to make your conclusion more creative than: • … and they lived happily ever after. • … and that is the story of … • … and that is the end of my story. • … and so, I guess I have nothing more to say. • … the end. Here are a few ways I end stories. • … and he ate both pieces of meat, wagging his broken tail. • … and as little Buttons put her head on her pillow, she smiled. Because in her imagination, she saw it all. • I am personally moved every time I tell this story. It shows how a Gentile like me can approach the God of Jacob, Isaac, and Abraham. I may ramble in different directions throughout the middle of these stories, but I always come back to the preplanned ending. 2. The story ending finding you Sometimes a story will create its own natural ending, and it comes to you while you are telling the story. It is usually better than the one you planned to use. Learn to recognize a natural ending, and when this happens, stop talking! A common mistake among storytellers is the story ends, and they keep talking. 3. Abrupt story ending The opposite is also a problem, and one I often make. I tend to end my story abruptly without giving my audience adequate preparation. It is usually best to let people know the story is about to end. Still, a little abruptness is better than going on and on. 4. Story ending as told with body language Ending a story involves more than words. Making a story memorable requires that you create a mood that will stay with the audience after you have finished. The mood of a story is created by pauses, vocal inflections, body language, etc. A good ending protects and enhances the mood; a bad ending can destroy it. As I approach the end of a story, I drop my voice a little (but not too much), slow my pace, and say each word distinctly. After the last word, I stand quietly for a few seconds, take a small step back, and bow my head slightly. My ending is simple, yet definite. It maintains the mood of the story without detracting from the message. Every storyteller has a different way of doing this, but usually they are consistent in how they do it. So here is your homework. Watch other storytellers and observe how they end their stories. Soon you will easily create your own style of ending a story. 5. Make the story tighter The most common critique given to all storytellers is, "You need to tighten it up." Often a poor story would be excellent if told in half the time. This is especially true of personal stories. Going on and on about something does not require a particular talent. It takes skill to tighten up a story so it is more pointed. One way to do this is have a definite, preplanned ending.

9

Life has meaning only in the struggle.

A boy grows up poor, raised by a single mother who struggles with alcoholism and is prone to violence. He finds fame and fortune and becomes a millionaire in his twenties. The good times end and he goes broke. He is forced to live in a tiny studio apartment, washing his dishes in the bathtub. The man regains his fortune, and then some. Today he walks with royalty. For the princely retainer of $1 million a year, he advises kings and queens, presidents and prime ministers, celebrities and business leaders. He has traded that tiny apartment for a 300-acre resort on the north side of Fiji. If you haven't guessed by now, the story's protagonist is motivational guru Tony Robbins. At six foot seven inches, Robbins is a big man with a big mission: He calls himself a "hunter of human happiness." He's also one of the most successful public speakers of our time. Robbins's TED talk has garnered more than 14 million views, making it one of the top 10 talks in TED history. He brings energy and passion to his herculean 50-hour seminars, which have been attended by a combined 4 million people. Another 50 million people have purchased his books and audios. At the age of 55, Robbins is a motivational powerhouse, but he wasn't born that way. It was a single conversation that set Robbins on his quest for success. Robbins was writing a sports article for his high school yearbook when he got the opportunity to interview legendary sports anchor Howard Cosell. He asked Cosell what it takes to be a successful sports announcer. Cosell responded, "You have to learn to understand the art of communication, develop it in such a way that it will capture the attention of the greatest number of people." 1 Robbins took the advice and acted on it. At the urging of a teacher, he ran for student body president. Few people gave him a chance to win, but one wellcrafted speech to the student body propelled Robbins *ahead of the competition. Robbins's high school classmate Julie Fellinger was there when Robbins took the podium. "He spoke from the heart," 2 she recalls. "He told a personal story about himself, about his struggle growing up. It was very touching. It was very compelling. It was inspirational. He was elected student body president because of it." When Robbins was 11 years old, his family didn't have enough money to buy a Thanksgiving meal. A stranger knocked on the family's door and left groceries. Robbins never forgot the act of kindness and it influenced the charities he eventually started. More important to the topic of storytelling, Robbins soon realized that by sharing his personal pain, he could make a strong emotional connection with his listeners, many of whom at Los Angeles's Glendora High School in 1977 shared the same socioeconomic background. In that moment Robbins learned a fundamental lesson that separates the superachievers from everyone else. People who have experienced pain, poverty, struggle, or despair—and many of the storytellers in this book have experienced it all—are only empowered by their experience when they've developed the courage to embrace their backstory, learn from their failures, and share their lessons of struggle with others. The Storyteller's Tools "I always say, change your story change your life, because whatever your story is will become the shaper of your life," 3 Robbins says. The problem, Robbins believes, is that some people are addicted to reliving their story of pain until it becomes a mental prison, preventing them from fulfilling their potential. "Everybody has parts of their life that shape the way they look at today and how they behave today. Everyone has a backstory. They have multiple backstories. The question is, which one is running you now?" Robbins has consulted and interviewed the most successful people of our time: Bill Clinton, Nelson Mandela, Marc Benioff, and countless others. In his 30-year career of studying personal growth and development, Robbins has discovered that the most successful people share a backstory of struggle and it's the hunger to write a new story that drives them to overcome their limited circumstances. "If you ask 'what's the difference in human beings in the way they perform,' it's not intelligence or ability," 4 says Robbins. "Almost anyone we know who has done something they're proud of in their life or they feel good about in their life, had to get through the obstacles, their own limiting stories. They had to find something they wanted more. The hunger often comes from a story of frustration or pain or desire. Finding that touchstone and igniting it is how you can take someone who is not driven and hungry and really help them to change their life." Robbins taps into his hunger story to drive himself and to motivate others. A Google search for "Tony Robbins + 400 square foot apartment" will return more than 250,000 links. The story is common knowledge because Robbins* *doesn't hide from it. He embraces it and uses the pain he felt when he didn't have food to eat or a roof over his head to drive him forward. He also uses the story to connect with his audience. Success leaves clues and often those clues are right before your eyes. People simply want to know that it's possible for them to live a better life. Through his story, Robbins provides a living role model. If he can do it, so can I, they say to themselves. Robbins is a close friend of actor Sylvester Stallone, who has a similar story of struggle. When Stallone wrote the script for Rocky, producers bid up to $350,000 for the rights to the script, with the caveat that Stallone, whom they didn't see as a leading man, not play the lead. Stallone, who had $100 in his checkbook at the time, said no. "It's my story," 5 he said. He finally negotiated a deal to play the lead for $35,000 and a cut of the receipts. Rocky grossed $200 million. Stallone refused to sell the script as long as another actor played the title character because the story of a boxer was a metaphor for his personal life story. The Dramatic Arc A Hollywood movie producer once told me that the story of Rocky is one of the greatest films ever made because it has an irresistible dramatic arc. A skilled movie writer creates a character you want to root for, and Rocky Balboa was the very embodiment of this kind of character. The movie is divided into three parts. The first part of the film builds Rocky's backstory, the struggle he must experience on his road to redemption. Rocky isn't just down on his luck. He's a small-time boxer living in a dark, grimy apartment. He earns his living breaking thumbs for a loan shark. In the middle section of the movie we are introduced to the movie's emotional hook. Through a quirk of fate, Rocky Balboa gets a oncein-a-lifetime chance to fight the world champion, Apollo Creed. He trains hard, if unconventionally, punching sides of beef instead of punching bags and running up the steps of the Philadelphia Museum of Art, accompanied by Bill Conti's rousing musical score. By the time the audience reaches the third part of the movie—the fight and resolution—they are emotionally invested in seeing Rocky reach his goal, which, by the way, is not to win the fight. He just wants to go the distance. He succeeds and, as he embraces Adrian who stood by his side, it's nearly impossible for moviegoers to stay in their seats. They stand up and cheer for a fictional character because they have been transported into his life and they see something of themselves in his struggle. If he can do it, I can, too. The first rule of emotional moviemaking is to create scenes early in the film that put the hero's life into perspective. Audiences need to build a relationship with a character they like and whose struggle they recognize, otherwise they don't care about the resolution. Just as great movies have dramatic arcs that take the audience on a journey through struggle and redemption, so, too, do most successful storytellers on the business stage. They struggle, find strength* *in their struggle, and ultimately success or redemption. The greater the arc, the better the story. And the more likely it is to ignite the passion of an audience. In every public seminar Tony Robbins tells the story of his early struggle because the arc makes people emotionally invested in the outcome. The more dramatic, the more likely it is to ignite the passion of your audience. Some people in the audience may have experienced grinding poverty as Robbins did. Some who were brought up middle or upper class may have experienced the pain of a troubled parent or an event that left them demoralized and disillusioned. They are invested in his story because it's become their story. Nearly every person in this book has faced a significant personal challenge or struggle in their life and has overcome the struggle in part through communicating it and its lessons of empowerment. But make no mistake, the story of struggle they share with the world is only impactful because they've reframed it and embraced it themselves. We have all experienced seminal events in our lives. In some cases, like Tony Robbins, it's the experience of grinding poverty, but for you it might be something completely different, such as being turned down by your first choice college or being passed over for a job. You can embrace the event and use it as a growth experience, or allow the experience to run you, usually into the ground. Your potential is not rooted in your backstory; it's formed by how you interpret your backstory. The Storyteller's Secret Stories have the power to shape our lives and the lives of our listeners. Our personal experience—the stories we've lived through—makes us who we are today. Stories of overcoming obstacles provide a dramatic arc to the narrative we tell the world. Inspiring storytellers don't avoid the difficult parts of their arc, but rather embrace every step as an opportunity to transform, grow, and to make a deeply meaningful emotional connection with their audience.*

10

The Finishing Touches

Here is the thin line I told you about—the one that separates the fourteen steps into two parts. The first nine steps are basic for creating a great story. They are essential for developing your God-given method of communication. These nine steps help you relate your story to others. As I promised, you can now skip steps 10–14 and move on to the next section where I will teach you how to use storytelling tools. They will greatly enhance your newly improved skills. Steps 10 through 14 are not for everyone. They are for those who want to learn the true joy of storytelling. If you decide to continue on with steps 10–14, be prepared for a great adventure! CUT AND PASTE This is the cut-and-paste part. I become a little sensitive about my story when I'm asked to use scissors on it. I'm sure I'm not alone. Take Jim. He labored over his Bible story and took all nine steps to this point. He's confident he doesn't need to cut and paste. His wife agrees and says he does such a good job telling it. His mother is proud and says the story is great—just the way it is. He is certain that any further changes would ruin what he's worked so hard to accomplish. Then there is Kim. She has put together a personal story that relates an emotional time in her family. She feels it is too precious to cut and paste. Her husband is moved to tears whenever he hears her tell it. He assures Kim that changing anything about it would be a mistake. The head of the women's ministry at their church says Kim could tell the story at the next women's retreat. Sorry, Jim and Kim. Together we are going to take your super stories and make changes. But when we're done you'll be amazed at how much they have improved. STEP 10: Research the Facts It is natural to think that researching the facts would come sooner in the crafting process. But there is a reason it is step 10. If you had done it earlier, the research would have greatly influenced how the story sounded. It would have hindered you from making it relevant to presentday concerns. The story needed to flow freely in the early stages of development without being hampered by ... uh ... well ... without being hampered by the facts. HIT THE BOOKS Your story is now ready for the facts. Besides, it needs a little spice. There is a world of information that will give you facts about your story and provide insights that will enhance the finished product. It will provide you great material your audience will find fascinating. But be careful. Cultural understanding, historical facts, national customs, and family history are like salt and pepper for a good meal. You would never serve food with an inch of salt on top. Instead, you use it sparingly to add spice and interest to the meal. Too much information will turn a story into a lecture. Compared to the 100 percent of the research material you'll gather, you will only use about 2 percent of it. Oh, but don't let that worry you. That 2 percent will add so much spice to your story, you won't mind the work you put into it. Besides, the other 98 percent will be used in future stories. FOLKTALES If you are telling a folktale, research various aspects of it. Possibly look into the background of the story, the customs of the main characters, or the occupations talked about. In "A Girl and Her Dreams," there are several things that may seem strange to us today. How did a dairy farm operate in former times? How did women carry heavy things on their heads? What did the town market look like and how was business carried on? How did farm people perform their chores? The questions go on and on. BIBLE STORIES If you're telling a Bible story, now is the time to look into the commentaries, Bible atlas, Bible dictionary, and biblical times and culture books. For instance, let's say you're preparing a story on Matthew 17:24–27 about the fish with a coin in its mouth. Peter had been asked if his master paid the temple tax. He didn't know how to respond. Later Jesus brought up the issue. The Lord told Peter to go to the Sea of Galilee and catch a fish. The first fish he caught had a coin in its mouth, which was used to pay the tax. When you come to step 10, look into your study resources. You may want to check The New Manners and Customs of Bible Times by Ralph Gower. You will be surprised to learn that the miracle was not that the fish had a coin in its mouth. That type of fish often has a shiny object in its mouth. When the female fish lays her eggs, she carries them in her mouth as an incubator. In time, the eggs hatch, but the little ones continue to live in Mom's mouth. One day the little fish swim out and Mom doesn't let them back in. At that point, she suffers from "empty nest syndrome," so she goes to the bottom of the lake and picks up a shiny object to carry in her mouth. This can be a piece of metal, a shiny stone, or a coin. The miracle was not the fish, but the fishing. The Lord knew the next catch would be a fish with a coin in its mouth. He also knew the coin would be enough to pay the tax for Him and Peter. This type of information is invaluable and adds greater understanding to the story. PERSONAL STORIES If you're telling a personal story, talk to others who were also at the event. Let's say you're preparing a story about a vacation your family took when you were a child. Your memories are clear about what happened. So your story should be based on your recollection of the facts. Once you get to step 10, talk to other members of the family who were on the same trip. You will be amazed how each of them will recall the experience differently. Their recollections are influenced by what was happening in their lives at the time. What you hear will make you think they are talking about a totally different trip. In addition, they will remind you of things you had forgotten. They will also give you added insight about that vacation from their viewpoint. But be careful. Don't allow them to convince you that your memories are wrong. You will eventually get more than enough information. Remember, you are only going to use a little of it in your story—to add flavor. GIVE IT A TRY: Now, let's apply this to the story we are working on together. Go to the computer and do some research that relates to "A Girl and Her Dreams." Find out everything you can about the time in history when the story may have happened. Because this story is ageless, you may have to select a time period of your liking. Look up some of the things we mentioned on the previous page. Once you feel you have enough information, take a little of it and sprinkle it into your story. STEP 11: Eliminate Needless Details You may be happy with how your story has developed so far, but it is about to get better. The next two steps will change how intently the audience listens as you tell your story. Here is the key: a story that captivates an audience is one-third details and two-thirds description. To give perspective to this principle, imagine you have a story that is fifteen minutes long. For it to be a tremendous story, you must be able to tell the essential facts in five minutes. Ten minutes should be given to pauses, facial expressions, body movements, and (most important) description. Step 11 eliminates needless details. Step 12 adds in the description. So it is time to get rid of a lot of details so you have room for description. These are the types of details that must go: ACCURACY DETAILS I heard a friend tell a fascinating story about a dog he had as a child. We laughed until we cried as we heard about the antics of that dog. Later I asked, "Did all of that really happen in one week?" He smiled and gave me a sheepish look. "No, John, it happened over three years. But if I had told all the details, no one would have been interested in the story." He was right. It was immaterial that the dog did those things over three years. It was more important for us to enter into this man's childhood and see the close relationship he had with his dog. The purpose was for us to remember a pet we had as a child and once again feel the warmth that an animal brought to our souls. Accuracy details would have distracted us from that purpose. I am not advocating lying, but your audience doesn't need to know everything that happened. In fact, they don't want to know everything that happened. It is not important to get all the particulars straight. This would include: who sat where, what they wore, who said what in what order, what day it was, and the precise sequence of events. Learn to leave some of these details unsaid. PERSONAL DETAILS Once I heard a missionary present his work to a church. He gave many personal details, most of which meant nothing to the audience. Everyone was wondering why the pastor had given up the pulpit to this man. I visited with the missionary later and he expressed his despair about the apathy of American people toward missions. "I spent my whole life on the mission field, and no one seems to care." He didn't realize the problem was his presentation. A few weeks later I heard another missionary relate stories about her mission work in Papua New Guinea. Everyone paid close attention as they listened to every word. They laughed at certain parts, and were moved to tears at others. Later I learned that a storytelling coach had taught her how to tell stories and craft captivating presentations. He helped her eliminate all the meaningless personal details. She carefully learned the skills of storytelling and perfected a presentation that is one of the most effective I have heard. EMOTIONAL DETAILS Be careful you don't get overcome with emotions while telling a story. Bear in mind, showing emotions in a story is a good thing, but it needs to be approached with care. Before you tell a personal story, you need to honestly evaluate your emotional control. You may find this is not the right time to share certain experiences. If you are not able to control your emotions, be aware of the following. · You will tend to make your presentation too long. You won't notice the audience growing impatient as you tell them details they don't want to hear. · You will violate their trust. Most people don't know how to react when a speaker starts crying uncontrollably. Their embarrassment will not help you find the healing you need. Still, storytelling is great therapy if you are hurting emotionally and need to vent feelings. But it has to be done right. Here are a few guidelines. · Contact a small group of people who love you and understand the circumstances. · Prepare them for what you are going to do. · Make sure they will appreciate all the details you are about to share. · Everyone should know your situation well enough that if you break down and cry, they are crying with you. · Invite them to interrupt you at any time and express their feelings or ask questions about what they don't understand. · You still need to have sufficient composure to continue and finish the story. · If you are emotionally able, allow comments and feedback afterward. GIVE IT A TRY: Now let's get back to the story we are working on together. This is one of the times you can tell your story to yourself. See how much you can shorten it without taking away from the message. What little details can you get rid of? What information is unnecessary? Tell the story in as short a time as you can. This is only an activity. Later you may find you need to put some of these details back in the story. I often go overboard here and take too much out. But for now, pare down the story. You are going to need the room. STEP 12: Add Description to the Story "I love the feeling of being inside the story." This was in an email I received from a teenager who attended one of my storytelling concerts. There are two distinct types of description that need to be added to your story—the five senses and emotions. THE FIVE SENSES A story needs to stimulate the five senses of those who are listening. This draws a person into the story. There should be enough description so the audience will see, hear, taste, smell, and feel everything going on. The old storytelling principle says, "Never state a fact if you can bring that fact to life." I walked into my mother's kitchen. Oh, it reminded me of when I was a boy. I immediately smelled the hot biscuits Mom had just brought out of the oven. I kissed her at the same time I reached for a biscuit. "Ouch! They're hot." "You leave those alone. They're for breakfast." Ignoring her, I broke open the captured biscuit. Steam rose up from both halves. The butter melted away as soon as it touched them. I quickly spread on some of Mom's homemade jam. She just smiled but still acted like she was upset with me. As soon as I bit into that delicious biscuit, flavor exploded into my mouth. Oh, it is good to be home again! Go through this little memory and identify each of the five senses. Do you see how this might be better than "I went home to visit my parents, and enjoyed eating one of Mom's biscuits"? Most stories are told using only the senses of sight and sound, leaving out taste, smell, and touch. Sight and sound are necessary, but they are lighter. The last three are heavier and make the greatest impact on the listener. You will be amazed how much your storytelling will improve if you just add in a little of these. Bedtime stories will be much more exciting. Business presentations will be more interesting. Counseling sessions will be more meaningful. People will find themselves "inside the story." EMOTIONS Description is not factual information. It is feelings and emotions that help the listener enter the world of the story. It is taking an ordinary action statement and expanding it. Description transforms statements of fact into exciting life experiences. Remember: People don't want to listen to your story; they want to experience it. I stand at the free throw line with the ball in my hand. I feel so alone in a room filled with yelling onlookers. I bounce the ball three times as I always do. The sweat rolls down the back of my neck. We are one point from winning the championship, and the ending buzzer has sounded. If I make this basket, our team will win and I will be carried off the court in triumph. Parents will name their children after me. But ... but if I miss *this one ... the fans will turn into an angry mob. A security guard will hide me in a closet and sneak me out under the cover of night. Our family will have to move to a different city. The players of both teams look at me from the two sides of the court. I see looks of hope, pain, jeers, glares, encouragement, and disdain. I bounce the ball two more times. I know my girlfriend is watching. If I make this basket, she will love me forever. But ... if I miss, I will never see her again. Oh, I know that Bill Jenkins is moving in her direction right now, hoping I'll miss this shot. The referee glares at me as if to say, "Shoot the stupid ball! My dinner is waiting." I lift the ball into the air and stretch. The tension of my whole body flows out through my fingertips. With a jerk I let the ball leave my hands.... It arches high, moving toward the basket as if in slow motion. It's ... it's ... it's ... Go through this little memory and identify all of the emotions. Do you see how this might be better than "I shot the basket at the free throw line"? GIVE IT A TRY: Three-step exercise Step one—Here is a simple action phrase: "I put on my shoes." Take two full minutes to describe the action of putting on your shoes. Add in as many senses and emotions as you can. Don't worry. No one is listening. Wait! Don't skip over this step. I know it seems a bit strange. But for a two-minute investment, you can greatly improve your storytelling skill that will last you for the rest of your life. When you apply this technique to a story, you strengthen its character and add depth of meaning. Step two—Select a simple phrase in your story "A Girl and Her Dreams." Take two full minutes to describe the action. Don't worry. You won't keep that in your telling. This is only an exercise. Step three—If you have done your homework and eliminated needless details, you are ready to add in valuable descriptions. Go to your designated listener and tell your story using the tools of the five senses and emotions. Extra credit—Once you have told your story to your designated listener, tell it two more times to other people. You will be amazed how it will develop through this process. But more than your story will develop. You are becoming a first-class storyteller! DEEP SILENCE Speakers often use humor in their presentations to gain reassurance that people are listening. They know their speech is going well if people laugh or smile. Intense description adds another dimension to how people listen. You will learn to gain reassurance through what I call "deep silence." Skilled storytellers listen for this when they are performing a story. When they first stand in front of an audience, there is a gentle rustling around the room. Once the story starts, the audience becomes quiet as their interest level increases. As the story intensifies, the crowd is no longer conscious of anything except events within the story. That is when deep silence happens. Once you learn to listen for it, you will never rely on any other form of reassurance. POWER OF THE STORY People don't make decisions based on facts they hear or even know. They make decisions based on what they have experienced. The purpose of being descriptive is to get people into the story where they will experience the heart of it. Stories impact lives. When you increase your ability to draw people into the heart of your story, you are increasing the impact your stories will have in their lives.*

11

comfortable speaking to an audience

Here are three precautions to remember as you prepare to get your audience to participate. The activity should fit the story. Make sure the activities you use are natural and fit the stories. Make the participation seem so effortless that the listener could not imagine the story without it. In "Tricky Raccoon," I have some children volunteer to represent the elements of weather and others represent the animals involved. All the other children are singing the repeating song and giving answers to my questions. It seems chaotic to others, but the activities fit the story and keep everyone's interest at a high pitch. The activity should fit the audience. Make sure the activity fits your audience's age group. For adults to participate, they need to think, I can imagine myself doing this. It fits the story, it is appropriate, and it will help make the story more complete. The audience participation in a story entitled "Dry Fry" fits the story so well that even the most unresponsive adults in the room will chime in "Everybody knows Dry Fry" at the appropriate time. People usually specialize in one age group. That is normal. But be prepared. Somewhere down the line, you will be asked to tell a story to a different age group. Be prepared to switch gears and tell a different kind of story with different audience participation. Recently I was asked to tell stories and lead activities for children of a certain age. I prepared for that age group. I was shocked to see a class full of children who were much younger. For some reason I didn't switch my approach but decided to continue on as planned. That didn't last long! Even though I don't normally work with that younger crowd, I had to make drastic adjustments right in the middle of the program. The arrangement of stories should fit the audience. The way stories are placed in a program will differ according to the age of the audience. Children will sit and listen quietly to any story for a short amount of time. But as time goes on, they will grow bored if activities don't increase. Therefore, save your best participation stories until the end. With children, I start with the least exciting and move toward the most active. Conversely, if I have several stories to tell adults, I will start with the most active one. This helps them put aside the cares of their daily lives and draws them into the event. The more thought-provoking stories come later in the adult program, once they have concluded they are enjoying themselves. GIVE IT A TRY: I have given you several audience participation ideas. Experiment with one of them. Ask a spouse or friend to help you. Explain what you are doing and ask him/her to participate as you tell the story. STEP 14: Arrange Practice Audiences The only way to finalize your preparation is to tell your story in front of listeners. Storytelling is a form of communication between people. Practicing a story in front of a mirror doesn't count. Communication must be practiced in front of people. You already involved someone when you pushed through a story, and you practiced several storytelling techniques in front of your designated listener. It is only a small step to move on to a larger audience. I recommend a practice audience. For years I told all my new stories at a retirement home in my town. They understood what I was doing, and they were willing to be my practice audience. They knew I was not telling them polished stories. So after I finished telling my stories, a small group would stay behind to appraise the story and give me suggestions. To this day, I value the input they gave me. By the way, they became my biggest fans. If I was telling stories to a public audience anywhere in town, my critique group would organize transportation and come to see how well I had listened to their advice. Find your own practice audience. A partial list of possibilities would include family get-togethers, retirement homes, libraries, schools, day care centers, Sunday school classes, youth groups, and storytelling/coaching groups. CREATE A COACHING GROUP The retirement home I mentioned was a coaching group for me, but I was the only storyteller being critiqued. You should also create (or join) a coaching group that includes other storytellers wanting to develop their skills. This could be people from only one organization, or it could include others as well. There may already be a storytelling guild in your area. They would be pleased if you decided to join them. If you start a coaching group, it is important to set guidelines that control the amount of criticism given. Here are tips I picked up from my good friend Don Falkos, a storytelling coach from Madison, Wisconsin. He uses levels A, B, C, D when he coaches—Attending, Bravos, Clarifications, Direction. Level 1: Attending—A person tells the story and the audience simply gives their attention. At this level, the storyteller gets up, tells the story, the audience applauds, and the storyteller sits down. This is THE most important step in the process. This is called "Attending" but it is much more than just paying attention. Don says, "The coach is to listen, really listen! This listening is not so we can respond. No. We listen in order to understand." Level 2: Bravos —The teller hears compliments about what was really good in the story. There are times when the storyteller wants input but is not ready for criticism. Receiving appreciation about the story is especially valuable to a storyteller. It is the second most valuable part of this process. I will quote Don here. We have a tendency to tell storytellers what they're doing wrong —so they can fix it. It is much more helpful to acknowledge what they are doing well. They may not realize these things unless someone tells them. These comments are to be statements of fact or experience. "That was funny." "Your story moved me." "I liked how you portrayed the various characters in the story both vocally and physically." "You used the space around you very effectively." These are all statements of fact from the perspective of those who are coaching. Level 3: Clarifications—Time for asking questions—in both directions. This level builds the rapport between the storyteller and audience. It also reduces the possibility of offense that might happen during the final level. —Questions the storyteller might ask: The storyteller asks questions to determine whether or not they were clear in what they said. "Did you understand what I meant by …" "What did you think of …" "Was it clear what the character was thinking when …" —Questions the audience might ask: People in the audience ask questions to determine whether or not to make a particular suggestion. "Why did you use that particular voice for your grandfather?" "Explain that section where …" "What did you mean when you said …" Level 4: Direction—Receiving advice on weak areas. I will quote Don again: This is where we excel—or so we assume. We think we know what will work best for the other person's story. But that's not so. Only the storyteller can know what is best for the story. The job of the coach is to guide the storyteller on a path of discovery. Oh, I know. It is much easier to simply tell the storyteller how to improve the story, instead of allowing the storyteller to make the discovery. But the simple fact is, the coach doesn't need to know "what is best" in order to be a help. The comments given to the storyteller are subjective statements and the storyteller has no obligation to accept them at face value. These suggestions reflect what the coach thinks would be helpful. Often the coach is wrong. One thing I really like about this level is the domino effect. One person offers a suggestion that is worthless. But that suggestion sparks a thought in someone else. That person makes a different suggestion that is also worthless. But that person's suggestion sparks a thought in yet another person. It is their suggestion that turns out to be exactly what the storyteller needs. I often say, "Everything you need as a storyteller is already inside you. You just need a little help to find it." AT THE MONTHLY MEETING Generally, each person should be allowed ten to twelve minutes in which to tell a story. Exceptions to this rule can be made if arranged in advance. If your story is longer than twelve minutes, select one part you will tell the group. It is not necessary to hear an entire story for the group to get a sense of how it flows. Appoint a timekeeper who has the authority to interrupt the teller when the time is up. A little flexibility should be given; especially if it is obvious the story is near the end. The timekeeper can also tell the storyteller the length of the story, which is a valuable piece of information. Another idea for your monthly meeting is to begin each session with a tip from this book. Make sure it does not last longer than ten minutes. There will always be business that the coaching group needs to address. I recommend selecting officers who are in charge of such business and having them meet at a different time. ANNUAL STORYTELLING EVENTS The main purpose of the group is for members to receive help for their stories and encourage other storytellers. Still, once the group has worked together for a while, they may want to conduct a storytelling concert. This has the same effect on a storyteller as a recital has on a musician. It also provides a fun event appropriate for people in your area. TAKING STOCK We have just gone through fourteen steps for crafting a story. I trust these suggestions will enhance your ability to tell stories, make presentations, conduct workshops, and teach God's message. Communication is a skill that can be learned. This is done one step at a time. With the crafting process in place, it is time to move on to the presentation of the story. We will now turn our attention to some basic storytelling tools.

12

creating a great story

Here is the thin line I told you about—the one that separates the fourteen steps into two parts. The first nine steps are basic for creating a great story. They are essential for developing your God-given method of communication. These nine steps help you relate your story to others. As I promised, you can now skip steps 10–14 and move on to the next section where I will teach you how to use storytelling tools. They will greatly enhance your newly improved skills. Steps 10 through 14 are not for everyone. They are for those who want to learn the true joy of storytelling. If you decide to continue on with steps 10–14, be prepared for a great adventure! CUT AND PASTE This is the cut-and-paste part. I become a little sensitive about my story when I'm asked to use scissors on it. I'm sure I'm not alone. Take Jim. He labored over his Bible story and took all nine steps to this point. He's confident he doesn't need to cut and paste. His wife agrees and says he does such a good job telling it. His mother is proud and says the story is great—just the way it is. He is certain that any further changes would ruin what he's worked so hard to accomplish. Then there is Kim. She has put together a personal story that relates an emotional time in her family. She feels it is too precious to cut and paste. Her husband is moved to tears whenever he hears her tell it. He assures Kim that changing anything about it would be a mistake. The head of the women's ministry at their church says Kim could tell the story at the next women's retreat. Sorry, Jim and Kim. Together we are going to take your super stories and make changes. But when we're done you'll be amazed at how much they have improved. STEP 10: Research the Facts It is natural to think that researching the facts would come sooner in the crafting process. But there is a reason it is step 10. If you had done it earlier, the research would have greatly influenced how the story sounded. It would have hindered you from making it relevant to presentday concerns. The story needed to flow freely in the early stages of development without being hampered by ... uh ... well ... without being hampered by the facts. HIT THE BOOKS Your story is now ready for the facts. Besides, it needs a little spice. There is a world of information that will give you facts about your story and provide insights that will enhance the finished product. It will provide you great material your audience will find fascinating. But be careful. Cultural understanding, historical facts, national customs, and family history are like salt and pepper for a good meal. You would never serve food with an inch of salt on top. Instead, you use it sparingly to add spice and interest to the meal. Too much information will turn a story into a lecture. Compared to the 100 percent of the research material you'll gather, you will only use about 2 percent of it. Oh, but don't let that worry you. That 2 percent will add so much spice to your story, you won't mind the work you put into it. Besides, the other 98 percent will be used in future stories. FOLKTALES If you are telling a folktale, research various aspects of it. Possibly look into the background of the story, the customs of the main characters, or the occupations talked about. In "A Girl and Her Dreams," there are several things that may seem strange to us today. How did a dairy farm operate in former times? How did women carry heavy things on their heads? What did the town market look like and how was business carried on? How did farm people perform their chores? The questions go on and on. BIBLE STORIES If you're telling a Bible story, now is the time to look into the commentaries, Bible atlas, Bible dictionary, and biblical times and culture books. For instance, let's say you're preparing a story on Matthew 17:24–27 about the fish with a coin in its mouth. Peter had been asked if his master paid the temple tax. He didn't know how to respond. Later Jesus brought up the issue. The Lord told Peter to go to the Sea of Galilee and catch a fish. The first fish he caught had a coin in its mouth, which was used to pay the tax. When you come to step 10, look into your study resources. You may want to check The New Manners and Customs of Bible Times by Ralph Gower. You will be surprised to learn that the miracle was not that the fish had a coin in its mouth. That type of fish often has a shiny object in its mouth. When the female fish lays her eggs, she carries them in her mouth as an incubator. In time, the eggs hatch, but the little ones continue to live in Mom's mouth. One day the little fish swim out and Mom doesn't let them back in. At that point, she suffers from "empty nest syndrome," so she goes to the bottom of the lake and picks up a shiny object to carry in her mouth. This can be a piece of metal, a shiny stone, or a coin. The miracle was not the fish, but the fishing. The Lord knew the next catch would be a fish with a coin in its mouth. He also knew the coin would be enough to pay the tax for Him and Peter. This type of information is invaluable and adds greater understanding to the story. PERSONAL STORIES If you're telling a personal story, talk to others who were also at the event. Let's say you're preparing a story about a vacation your family took when you were a child. Your memories are clear about what happened. So your story should be based on your recollection of the facts. Once you get to step 10, talk to other members of the family who were on the same trip. You will be amazed how each of them will recall the experience differently. Their recollections are influenced by what was happening in their lives at the time. What you hear will make you think they are talking about a totally different trip. In addition, they will remind you of things you had forgotten. They will also give you added insight about that vacation from their viewpoint. But be careful. Don't allow them to convince you that your memories are wrong. You will eventually get more than enough information. Remember, you are only going to use a little of it in your story—to add flavor. GIVE IT A TRY: Now, let's apply this to the story we are working on together. Go to the computer and do some research that relates to "A Girl and Her Dreams." Find out everything you can about the time in history when the story may have happened. Because this story is ageless, you may have to select a time period of your liking. Look up some of the things we mentioned on the previous page. Once you feel you have enough information, take a little of it and sprinkle it into your story. STEP 11: Eliminate Needless Details You may be happy with how your story has developed so far, but it is about to get better. The next two steps will change how intently the audience listens as you tell your story. Here is the key: a story that captivates an audience is one-third details and two-thirds description. To give perspective to this principle, imagine you have a story that is fifteen minutes long. For it to be a tremendous story, you must be able to tell the essential facts in five minutes. Ten minutes should be given to pauses, facial expressions, body movements, and (most important) description. Step 11 eliminates needless details. Step 12 adds in the description. So it is time to get rid of a lot of details so you have room for description. These are the types of details that must go: ACCURACY DETAILS I heard a friend tell a fascinating story about a dog he had as a child. We laughed until we cried as we heard about the antics of that dog. Later I asked, "Did all of that really happen in one week?" He smiled and gave me a sheepish look. "No, John, it happened over three years. But if I had told all the details, no one would have been interested in the story." He was right. It was immaterial that the dog did those things over three years. It was more important for us to enter into this man's childhood and see the close relationship he had with his dog. The purpose was for us to remember a pet we had as a child and once again feel the warmth that an animal brought to our souls. Accuracy details would have distracted us from that purpose. I am not advocating lying, but your audience doesn't need to know everything that happened. In fact, they don't want to know everything that happened. It is not important to get all the particulars straight. This would include: who sat where, what they wore, who said what in what order, what day it was, and the precise sequence of events. Learn to leave some of these details unsaid. PERSONAL DETAILS Once I heard a missionary present his work to a church. He gave many personal details, most of which meant nothing to the audience. Everyone was wondering why the pastor had given up the pulpit to this man. I visited with the missionary later and he expressed his despair about the apathy of American people toward missions. "I spent my whole life on the mission field, and no one seems to care." He didn't realize the problem was his presentation. A few weeks later I heard another missionary relate stories about her mission work in Papua New Guinea. Everyone paid close attention as they listened to every word. They laughed at certain parts, and were moved to tears at others. Later I learned that a storytelling coach had taught her how to tell stories and craft captivating presentations. He helped her eliminate all the meaningless personal details. She carefully learned the skills of storytelling and perfected a presentation that is one of the most effective I have heard. EMOTIONAL DETAILS Be careful you don't get overcome with emotions while telling a story. Bear in mind, showing emotions in a story is a good thing, but it needs to be approached with care. Before you tell a personal story, you need to honestly evaluate your emotional control. You may find this is not the right time to share certain experiences. If you are not able to control your emotions, be aware of the following. · You will tend to make your presentation too long. You won't notice the audience growing impatient as you tell them details they don't want to hear. · You will violate their trust. Most people don't know how to react when a speaker starts crying uncontrollably. Their embarrassment will not help you find the healing you need. Still, storytelling is great therapy if you are hurting emotionally and need to vent feelings. But it has to be done right. Here are a few guidelines. · Contact a small group of people who love you and understand the circumstances. · Prepare them for what you are going to do. · Make sure they will appreciate all the details you are about to share. · Everyone should know your situation well enough that if you break down and cry, they are crying with you. · Invite them to interrupt you at any time and express their feelings or ask questions about what they don't understand. · You still need to have sufficient composure to continue and finish the story. · If you are emotionally able, allow comments and feedback afterward. GIVE IT A TRY: Now let's get back to the story we are working on together. This is one of the times you can tell your story to yourself. See how much you can shorten it without taking away from the message. What little details can you get rid of? What information is unnecessary? Tell the story in as short a time as you can. This is only an activity. Later you may find you need to put some of these details back in the story. I often go overboard here and take too much out. But for now, pare down the story. You are going to need the room. STEP 12: Add Description to the Story "I love the feeling of being inside the story." This was in an email I received from a teenager who attended one of my storytelling concerts. There are two distinct types of description that need to be added to your story—the five senses and emotions. THE FIVE SENSES A story needs to stimulate the five senses of those who are listening. This draws a person into the story. There should be enough description so the audience will see, hear, taste, smell, and feel everything going on. The old storytelling principle says, "Never state a fact if you can bring that fact to life." I walked into my mother's kitchen. Oh, it reminded me of when I was a boy. I immediately smelled the hot biscuits Mom had just brought out of the oven. I kissed her at the same time I reached for a biscuit. "Ouch! They're hot." "You leave those alone. They're for breakfast." Ignoring her, I broke open the captured biscuit. Steam rose up from both halves. The butter melted away as soon as it touched them. I quickly spread on some of Mom's homemade jam. She just smiled but still acted like she was upset with me. As soon as I bit into that delicious biscuit, flavor exploded into my mouth. Oh, it is good to be home again! Go through this little memory and identify each of the five senses. Do you see how this might be better than "I went home to visit my parents, and enjoyed eating one of Mom's biscuits"? Most stories are told using only the senses of sight and sound, leaving out taste, smell, and touch. Sight and sound are necessary, but they are lighter. The last three are heavier and make the greatest impact on the listener. You will be amazed how much your storytelling will improve if you just add in a little of these. Bedtime stories will be much more exciting. Business presentations will be more interesting. Counseling sessions will be more meaningful. People will find themselves "inside the story." EMOTIONS Description is not factual information. It is feelings and emotions that help the listener enter the world of the story. It is taking an ordinary action statement and expanding it. Description transforms statements of fact into exciting life experiences. Remember: People don't want to listen to your story; they want to experience it. I stand at the free throw line with the ball in my hand. I feel so alone in a room filled with yelling onlookers. I bounce the ball three times as I always do. The sweat rolls down the back of my neck. We are one point from winning the championship, and the ending buzzer has sounded. If I make this basket, our team will win and I will be carried off the court in triumph. Parents will name their children after me. But ... but if I miss this one ... the fans will turn into an angry mob. A security guard will hide me in a closet and sneak me out under the cover of night. Our family will have to move to a different city. The players of both teams look at me from the two sides of the court. I see looks of hope, pain, jeers, glares, encouragement, and disdain. I bounce the ball two more times. I know my girlfriend is watching. If I make this basket, she will love me forever. But ... if I miss, I will never see her again. Oh, I know that Bill Jenkins is moving in her direction right now, hoping I'll miss this shot. The referee glares at me as if to say, "Shoot the stupid ball! My dinner is waiting." I lift the ball into the air and stretch. The tension of my whole body flows out through my fingertips. With a jerk I let the ball leave my hands.... It arches high, moving toward the basket as if in slow motion. It's ... it's ... it's ... Go through this little memory and identify all of the emotions. Do you see how this might be better than "I shot the basket at the free throw line"? GIVE IT A TRY: Three-step exercise Step one—Here is a simple action phrase: "I put on my shoes." Take two full minutes to describe the action of putting on your shoes. Add in as many senses and emotions as you can. Don't worry. No one is listening. Wait! Don't skip over this step. I know it seems a bit strange. But for a two-minute investment, you can greatly improve your storytelling skill that will last you for the rest of your life. When you apply this technique to a story, you strengthen its character and add depth of meaning. Step two—Select a simple phrase in your story "A Girl and Her Dreams." Take two full minutes to describe the action. Don't worry. You won't keep that in your telling. This is only an exercise. Step three—If you have done your homework and eliminated needless details, you are ready to add in valuable descriptions. Go to your designated listener and tell your story using the tools of the five senses and emotions. Extra credit—Once you have told your story to your designated listener, tell it two more times to other people. You will be amazed how it will develop through this process. But more than your story will develop. You are becoming a first-class storyteller! DEEP SILENCE Speakers often use humor in their presentations to gain reassurance that people are listening. They know their speech is going well if people laugh or smile. Intense description adds another dimension to how people listen. You will learn to gain reassurance through what I call "deep silence." Skilled storytellers listen for this when they are performing a story. When they first stand in front of an audience, there is a gentle rustling around the room. Once the story starts, the audience becomes quiet as their interest level increases. As the story intensifies, the crowd is no longer conscious of anything except events within the story. That is when deep silence happens. Once you learn to listen for it, you will never rely on any other form of reassurance. POWER OF THE STORY People don't make decisions based on facts they hear or even know. They make decisions based on what they have experienced. The purpose of being descriptive is to get people into the story where they will experience the heart of it. Stories impact lives. When you increase your ability to draw people into the heart of your story, you are increasing the impact your stories will have in their lives.

13

Last Ingredient

Each of the previous twelve steps is important, but the preparation process eventually requires an audience. Our final two steps will require a live audience. STEP 13: Include Audience Participation Not every story requires people to outwardly take part. But sometimes getting members of the audience to participate helps bring them into the story. This is especially important with children. The younger the listeners, the more active they should be in the telling of the story. When you become good at this, you will be able to keep a large number of children captivated with your story. But audience participation is not limited to children. Most adults are eager to get involved if you approach it right. It is amazingly easy to get them to participate. It is important they sense you are treating them like adults and not children. Chapter 14 is titled "Experiencing BibleTelling" and deals with adult audience participation in a Bible study setting. Activities vary according to the age of the audience and the personality of the storyteller. The most common is to have listeners say a repeating phrase or sing a repeating tune. A REPEATING SONG My favorite audience participation is a technique using little homemade songs. I am not a songwriter, so I simply think of a few words that fit the story and then sing it. It will take a few tries to make it smooth, but eventually it becomes a song I can use. It is usually a simple phrase like: Rapunzel, Rapunzel, let down your hair. Rapunzel, Rapunzel, let down your hair. I sing this little tune the first few times as I am telling the story. Eventually I have them singing it with me. Another way to use songs is to create a poem and put it to the tune of an old song. Here are some tunes that work well: • Home on the Range • Mary Had a Little Lamb • Bicycle Built for Two • On Top of Old Smokey • Row, Row, Row Your Boat • Take Me Out to the Ball Game • Clementine • Old MacDonald • The Farmer in the Dell REPEATING PHRASES A repeating phrase should be simple and recur throughout the story. Normally I don't prepare the audience for this. The first two times, I say it slowly and distinctly. The third time, I pause, move my hands toward the audience, cock my head, say it slowly, and half of the crowd joins in. The next time, everyone is saying it with me. With some repeating phrases, it is best to have the audience practice at the beginning of the tale. I usually say, "I need your help with this story. When I pause and hold out my hand, you say, 'Everyone knows Dry Fry!' Let's try it once." [Everyone knows Dry Fry!] "That was good. Let's try it one more time." [Everyone knows Dry Fry!] HAND MOTIONS Hand motions are effective and can be used for any age group. Just make sure the audience has ample warning. For instance, if they are to give a single clap at various points in the story, make sure you give them a signal that means "get ready to clap." Another idea is to learn a few signs from someone who knows sign language for the deaf. This can be educational and fun for your listeners. And the signs usually coordinate nicely with the phrase they communicate. USING VOLUNTEERS I like bringing volunteers to the front to help me illustrate the story. Children will always jump at the chance to come up front. If asked properly, adults will also cooperate. It takes courage the first time you do it, but you soon see how much people enjoy it. One caution: Be sensitive to those who don't want to participate. YOU'RE LIMITED ONLY BY YOUR CREATIVITY · I have had one side of the audience repeat a phrase that the other side echoes. · If you have objects that illustrate your story, have volunteers hold them for you. When you talk about each object, the designated person holds it up. · I have identified various locations within the story, and then placed them around the room. This opens many activities that can be done once you place volunteers at each location. · More ideas are in chapter 14. Watch others who are skilled in the area of audience participation. Talk to them and ask advice on how they developed their skill. Don't be afraid to try different techniques in front of various groups. It will bring more life to your stories, keep your listeners interested, and you will become more skilled as time goes on. THREE PRECAUTIONS Here are three precautions to remember as you prepare to get your audience to participate. The activity should fit the story. Make sure the activities you use are natural and fit the stories. Make the participation seem so effortless that the listener could not imagine the story without it. In "Tricky Raccoon," I have some children volunteer to represent the elements of weather and others represent the animals involved. All the other children are singing the repeating song and giving answers to my questions. It seems chaotic to others, but the activities fit the story and keep everyone's interest at a high pitch. The activity should fit the audience. Make sure the activity fits your audience's age group. For adults to participate, they need to think, I can imagine myself doing this. It fits the story, it is appropriate, and it will help make the story more complete. The audience participation in a story entitled "Dry Fry" fits the story so well that even the most unresponsive adults in the room will chime in "Everybody knows Dry Fry" at the appropriate time. People usually specialize in one age group. That is normal. But be prepared. Somewhere down the line, you will be asked to tell a story to a different age group. Be prepared to switch gears and tell a different kind of story with different audience participation. Recently I was asked to tell stories and lead activities for children of a certain age. I prepared for that age group. I was shocked to see a class full of children who were much younger. For some reason I didn't switch my approach but decided to continue on as planned. That didn't last long! Even though I don't normally work with that younger crowd, I had to make drastic adjustments right in the middle of the program. The arrangement of stories should fit the audience. The way stories are placed in a program will differ according to the age of the audience. Children will sit and listen quietly to any story for a short amount of time. But as time goes on, they will grow bored if activities don't increase. Therefore, save your best participation stories until the end. With children, I start with the least exciting and move toward the most active. Conversely, if I have several stories to tell adults, I will start with the most active one. This helps them put aside the cares of their daily lives and draws them into the event. The more thought-provoking stories come later in the adult program, once they have concluded they are enjoying themselves. GIVE IT A TRY: I have given you several audience participation ideas. Experiment with one of them. Ask a spouse or friend to help you. Explain what you are doing and ask him/her to participate as you tell the story. STEP 14: Arrange Practice Audiences The only way to finalize your preparation is to tell your story in front of listeners. Storytelling is a form of communication between people. Practicing a story in front of a mirror doesn't count. Communication must be practiced in front of people. You already involved someone when you pushed through a story, and you practiced several storytelling techniques in front of your designated listener. It is only a small step to move on to a larger audience. I recommend a practice audience. For years I told all my new stories at a retirement home in my town. They understood what I was doing, and they were willing to be my practice audience. They knew I was not telling them polished stories. So after I finished telling my stories, a small group would stay behind to appraise the story and give me suggestions. To this day, I value the input they gave me. By the way, they became my biggest fans. If I was telling stories to a public audience anywhere in town, my critique group would organize transportation and come to see how well I had listened to their advice. Find your own practice audience. A partial list of possibilities would include family get-togethers, retirement homes, libraries, schools, day care centers, Sunday school classes, youth groups, and storytelling/coaching groups. CREATE A COACHING GROUP The retirement home I mentioned was a coaching group for me, but I was the only storyteller being critiqued. You should also create (or join) a coaching group that includes other storytellers wanting to develop their skills. This could be people from only one organization, or it could include others as well. There may already be a storytelling guild in your area. They would be pleased if you decided to join them. If you start a coaching group, it is important to set guidelines that control the amount of criticism given. Here are tips I picked up from my good friend Don Falkos, a storytelling coach from Madison, Wisconsin. He uses levels A, B, C, D when he coaches—Attending, Bravos, Clarifications, Direction. Level 1: Attending—A person tells the story and the audience simply gives their attention. At this level, the storyteller gets up, tells the story, the audience applauds, and the storyteller sits down. This is THE most important step in the process. This is called "Attending" but it is much more than just paying attention. Don says, "The coach is to listen, really listen! This listening is not so we can respond. No. We listen in order to understand." Level 2: Bravos —The teller hears compliments about what was really good in the story. There are times when the storyteller wants input but is not ready for criticism. Receiving appreciation about the story is especially valuable to a storyteller. It is the second most valuable part of this process. I will quote Don here. We have a tendency to tell storytellers what they're doing wrong —so they can fix it. It is much more helpful to acknowledge what they are doing well. They may not realize these things unless someone tells them. These comments are to be statements of fact or experience. "That was funny." "Your story moved me." "I liked how you portrayed the various characters in the story both vocally and physically." "You used the space around you very effectively." These are all statements of fact from the perspective of those who are coaching. Level 3: Clarifications—Time for asking questions—in both directions. This level builds the rapport between the storyteller and audience. It also reduces the possibility of offense that might happen during the final level. —Questions the storyteller might ask: The storyteller asks questions to determine whether or not they were clear in what they said. "Did you understand what I meant by ..." "What did you think of ..." "Was it clear what the character was thinking when ..." —Questions the audience might ask: People in the audience ask questions to determine whether or not to make a particular suggestion. "Why did you use that particular voice for your grandfather?" "Explain that section where ..." "What did you mean when you said ..." Level 4: Direction—Receiving advice on weak areas.

I will quote Don again: This is where we excel—or so we assume. We think we know what will work best for the other person's story. But that's not so. Only the storyteller can know what is best for the story. The job of the coach is to guide the storyteller on a path of discovery. Oh, I know. It is much easier to simply tell the storyteller how to improve the story, instead of allowing the storyteller to make the discovery. But the simple fact is, the coach doesn't need to know "what is best" in order to be a help. The comments given to the storyteller are subjective statements and the storyteller has no obligation to accept them at face value. These suggestions reflect what the coach thinks would be helpful. Often the coach is wrong. One thing I really like about this level is the domino effect. One person offers a suggestion that is worthless. But that suggestion sparks a thought in someone else. That person makes a different suggestion that is also worthless. But that person's suggestion sparks a thought in yet another person. It is their suggestion that turns out to be exactly what the storyteller needs. I often say, "Everything you need as a storyteller is already inside you. You just need a little help to find it." AT THE MONTHLY MEETING Generally, each person should be allowed ten to twelve minutes in which to tell a story. Exceptions to this rule can be made if arranged in advance. If your story is longer than twelve minutes, select one part you will tell the group. It is not necessary to hear an entire story for the group to get a sense of how it flows. Appoint a timekeeper who has the authority to interrupt the teller when the time is up. A little flexibility should be given; especially if it is obvious the story is near the end. The timekeeper can also tell the storyteller the length of the story, which is a valuable piece of information. Another idea for your monthly meeting is to begin each session with a tip from this book. Make sure it does not last longer than ten minutes. There will always be business that the coaching group needs to address. I recommend selecting officers who are in charge of such business and having them meet at a different time. ANNUAL STORYTELLING EVENTS The main purpose of the group is for members to receive help for their stories and encourage other storytellers. Still, once the group has worked together for a while, they may want to conduct a storytelling concert. This has the same effect on a storyteller as a recital has on a musician. It also provides a fun event appropriate for people in your area. TAKING STOCK We have just gone through fourteen steps for crafting a story. I trust these suggestions will enhance your ability to tell stories, make presentations, conduct workshops, and teach God's message. Communication is a skill that can be learned. This is done one step at a time. With the crafting process in place, it is time to move on to the presentation of the story. We will now turn our attention to some basic storytelling tools.

14

You're looking out the window again

———❤———

You're not paying attention." It was true; I was looking out the school window but not at the trees. Everyone else in the classroom had missed it, but I saw it all. I saw those pioneer wagons moving through the tall, dry prairie grass. I could see that the grass was higher than a man sitting on a horse. It was dangerous this time of year because everything was so dry. The men kept their eyes on the horizon. Suddenly the entire wagon train heard the cry, "Fire! Fire!" The smell of smoke was heavy in the air. Off in the distance, the prairie was ablaze. With this strong wind, it wouldn't take long for the fire to reach us. I jumped out of the lead wagon, ready to help. With a sharp eye, I scanned the group and saw that everyone else was in hopeless panic. It was obvious I had to take charge. I ran downwind and pulled out a book of matches. Well ... uh ... no, we didn't have matches.... That's all right; I didn't need them anyway. I started hitting two rocks together, hoping to produce sparks. If I could get a break fire going, I could burn off some grass downwind of the wagons. Then the men could help me turn the wagon train around, and pull it on to the burnt area. I could save the lives of everyone and be a hero if I could just get the break fire going. Some of the women saw what I was doing but didn't understand. They were confused as to why I was starting a fire—when fire was the problem. They came running at me crying in heightened panic. One of them stood over me with a stern look on her face. "John! ... John! ... You're looking out the window again. You're not paying attention," my teacher repeated. In countless replays of this scene, my imagination got me in trouble when I was in school. Now I use it as a tool to communicate with my listeners more effectively. We were created with an ability to picture things in our minds. We can see history, the future, and ideas as if they exist in the present. In our minds, we can see things that do not exist and experience them as if they were real. Tool #1: Imagination To properly tell a story, you must see it in your mind. This ability to "see the story" requires a developed imagination. The more you are able to see the story, the less you will feel the need to memorize it. God has given us the gift of imagination. Like so many of God's gifts, it was created for good but is often wrongfully used or neglected. Many people allow their imaginations to be underdeveloped and lie dormant. I am going to help you develop this gift from God so you can use it to communicate with others. Oh, I know your imagination may not be as strong as others. So think of it as a foreign language. Others learn it quickly, but some have to practice more before they can master it. God made each of us unique, and He works with us individually. Second Corinthians 10:12 says it is not wise to compare ourselves with others. So let's strengthen your imagination muscle. Here are several exercises that will help. I got most of these from my friend Brian Fox Ellis, a professional storyteller in Peoria, Illinois. GIVE IT A TRY: Pick up an imaginary blob. Once you are holding it, don't let it disappear until you put it down again. Look at each of the following items. Imagine each one, and then carefully shape it with your imaginary blob. After it is shaped, use it in its most common way. · fishing pole · violin · apple · toothbrush · glass of water For the next few days observe your hands and your actions as you do common, everyday activities. When no one is watching, reenact the movements with nothing in your hands. Once when I was speaking at a church, I described a man with an opened umbrella. After the service, a lady commented that when I was finished with the illustration, I released the tension on the imaginary umbrella and put it away. I didn't remember doing this, but I understood why I did it. In my mind I saw the umbrella and used it as if it were real. Umbrellas don't just vanish, so I put it away when I was finished with it. Choose a simple happening and make a wordless story out of it. Do this slowly so you can think through every action. Don't allow anything to simply disappear. Allow enough space between your fingers when holding something. Also, think of how your body reacts when you do the activity. For instance, you might normally wiggle your toes when you put on your socks. The following list will help you get started: · brushing teeth · combing hair · driving a car · shaving · putting on clothes · making a sandwich Few presentations require a great amount of direct pantomiming. Still, as you tell a story, you will reach out a hand and pick up an imaginary object or brush aside something in your character's way. Since you will do this without thinking it must look real. I conducted a BibleTelling trip to Israel. A group of us told 110 Bible stories at the forty-five sites where they happened. I was with the group overlooking the valley where the Philistines returned the Ark of the Covenant, which they had stolen (1 Samuel 4–6). They had put the Ark on a new cart and hooked it up to two milk cows. The cows pulled the cart north until they came to the valley where we were standing. As I told that story, I came to the part where the Ark entered the valley. I subconsciously pointed to the entrance of the valley. I didn't plan on doing that, but in my imagination I saw the Ark and couldn't help but point at it. As soon as I did, the story was alive and visual for those standing on that hill. Instantly, everyone in the group saw the cows, cart, and Ark moving up the valley. Ask the help of a friend whose house you have not been in. I'll call this friend Bill. Imagine you are standing at the front door of Bill's house. Ask him to give you instructions so you can go through the house to the master bedroom. Once you are there in your imagination, have him tell you how to get to the dresser. In your mind, get an object from the dresser and take it back to the front door. Don't ask for details about the inside of the house, but envision what it looks like. Once you have envisioned this trip through his home, describe to Bill what the inside of his house looks like. He should sit quietly and not correct you. Use the following questions as a guide for your description. If you didn't see one part in your imagination, pause, envision it, and then answer the questions. · What color was the front door? · Describe any sounds you heard when you walked inside. · What kind of floors did you see as you walked through the house? · Describe the various wall colors. · What smells did you notice? · Describe the window coverings. · Describe the pictures on the wall. · How neat was the house? · Did you see any toys? If so, describe them. · If there were stairs in the house, describe them. · What was the bedspread like? · Was the bed made? · Describe the bedroom floor, walls, and window coverings. · Were there any smells or sounds in the bedroom? · Describe the dresser. · Describe what else you noticed about the house. Once you are done describing the inside of his house, Bill can tell you how correct you were. Of course you didn't get it right, but it doesn't matter. The exercise is only to force you to describe what you saw when Bill gave you the instructions. It makes you use your imagination. Think through your story "A Girl and Her Dreams." Use your imagination and craft the story so the main character is a boy rather than a girl. The story becomes "A Boy and His Dreams." Recruit several others to help you with this next exercise. It requires that they be ready to participate. · Tell your story "A Girl and Her Dreams" or "A Boy and His Dreams." · Once the story is done, the group is to ask you questions about every part of the story. It goes: "Tell me more about [some part of the story]" (e.g., "Tell me more about the girl—what did she look like?" "Tell me more about the house where she lived."). · You shouldn't act surprised with any question. Act as if you meant to tell that part but forgot. · The key is to make up more of the story as you go along. I enjoy conducting this kind of activity. Once I had an audience full of questions. I answered each one with confidence and conviction, which encouraged more questions. It was as if they felt I had left so much out of the story. They wanted to know more. Finally one woman asked, "Are you making this up as you go along?" "Sure, the more you ask, the more I make up." "Oh my! I was believing every word!" Strangely, this didn't slow down the questions. Everyone wanted to know more of the story.

15

Commitment to your body

The leader tried everything he could do to quiet the roomful of children. The storyteller stood along the outer wall and watched the futile attempts at calming the children. He muttered, "What have I gotten myself into?" Finally it was time for the stories. The leader looked relieved at the opportunity to let someone else entertain the children. The storyteller took off his glasses, put them away, and moved to the front of a group of distracted children. He immediately began his story. The children only glanced at him out of curiosity, but when they did, they grew quiet. They saw the story come alive on the storyteller's face. The children watched as the plot unfolded with the moving of eyebrows, the changing of wrinkles on the forehead, the flashing of eyes. One moment they saw glee, then an expression of fear. They watched his face register anger, happiness, sorrow, grief, suspicion, weariness, surprise, relief, shock, and delight. The children's eyes were intent on his face, worried to look away lest they miss something. When the stories ended, the children erupted into applause. They had just spent forty minutes listening, watching, and experiencing a story. It had traveled to them from the storyteller's imagination through his face, hands, and body. It found a home in the imaginations of the children, where it would stay for years to come. A SURPRISING FACT Your greatest storytelling tools are those people can see as the plot unfolds, not what they hear. The more you commit your body to a story, the more effective you will be in communicating the message. Spoken words make up only 15 to 20 percent of a live storytelling performance. Yes, it's true. I've seen brilliant storytellers who did not move at all when they told stories. They have learned to compensate in other ways. Still, most storytellers use the following two body tools extensively. Tool #2: Facial Expressions One of the people I have trained to use BibleTelling is a condemned murderer who is serving a life sentence in a maximum-security prison in Louisiana. He is now a true man of God and has a tremendous ministry behind bars. One day he asked me, "John, why do you always take off your glasses before you tell a story. Wait!" he exclaimed. "I think I know why. It's your way of praying before you start. As you take them off slowly, you are placing yourself in the presence of God. Right?" "Uh, well … no. That sounds like a great reason, but that's not it." My friend was surprised. "Then what is it? Why do you take off your glasses?" There was no way I could lie to this godly man. "It's because my wife told me to always take my glasses off before I tell a story. She says it helps people to see my face better." Our faces communicate life and enthusiasm. As people sit and listen to you, they are looking at your face so they can interpret what you are saying. They need to see the story as well as hear it. Facial expressions also communicate the emotions of the characters. It helps show changing moods that rage inside a story. Words can't express some emotions. The face conveys inner conflicts and private thoughts. Writers must use pages of material to capture what a storyteller can convey by a simple look. BE QUIET AND LET YOUR FACE SPEAK The face can't be rushed if it's to do its job. Facial expressions reduce the number of words by half and say twice as much. Slow down your spoken words so your face can tell its part of the story. At times, stop talking. Your face has too much to say to be interrupted by your voice. In one of my stories, my face shows the main character mustering up false bravery. He suddenly has to do a courageous deed. Fear spreads over his face, and he swallows hard. He licks his dry lips to moisten a fear-evoked dry mouth. Panic has a firm hold, but he moves into action anyway. All of this is communicated with only ten words and a large amount of facial expression. Those ten words, in fact, occupy a secondary position in the story. As I said before, your greatest storytelling tools are those people can see as the plot unfolds. Most people worry they will overdo facial expressions. When one of their face muscles move slightly, they feel like neon lights are flashing across their face. They think, There, I did it. Everyone saw that. I hope I didn't look too silly. No, you didn't look silly because no one saw it! You must overdo facial expressions. Put them on as an actor puts on stage makeup. You may feel you have gone to the extreme and look silly, but believe me, you are only getting close to having enough facial expression. DRESS WITH "THE FACE" IN MIND When you step in front of an audience, be dressed in a way that does not distract from your face. I am not talking about modesty. That is a different issue. Consider these things. Focal Point: Dress in a way that causes the audience to focus on your face. Make sure your outfit is long enough, high enough, and loose enough. Others are allowed to dress any way they want, but you need to be professional and dress in a way that causes the listener's eyes to look at your face. Sleeves: I watched an older storyteller once, and all I could think about was the loose, flabby skin on her upper arms. She needed to cover that up. I watched a man tell a story, but my eyes kept going to the tattoos on his arms. Cover up anything that distracts people from looking at your face. Hair: I don't have much hair on the top of my head. Those who do should fix it so it outlines the face and does not detract from it. Comfortable shoes and clothes: Storytelling requires a lot of movement, so it is important to wear loose, comfortable clothing. A look of pain on your face should be part of the plot—not because of tight shoes or clothing. There are times when the occasion dictates that you dress formally. To do otherwise would distract from your story. Still, whenever possible, dress in a way that allows freedom of movement. GIVE IT A TRY: It is time to once again tell "A Girl and Her Dreams." This time, stand in front of a mirror and tell it slowly. Exaggerate your facial expression with every emotion. As you watch yourself, don't stop because of your fits of laughter. Tool #3: Body Movements No one likes to get up in front of people and do something that is out of their comfort zone. Believe me, improving body movements doesn't mean a person has to look silly; actually, it is just the opposite. The purpose of perfecting body language is to draw the listener's attention away from you. Becoming skilled at this storytelling tool will help them focus on your message. BE AWARE OF WHAT YOUR BODY IS TELLING PEOPLE In some cases, your words are trying to communicate one thing while your body is communicating something different. The audience is listening to what you say and comparing it to what they see. From your body language, they judge your abilities, sincerity, confidence level, likability, and truthfulness. More importantly, they use this measure to gauge the value of your message. Once I did a community concert that was sponsored by a local library. I started by telling my audience that all of my stories would be fictional. After the first story, a man asked me if it was a true story. I reminded everyone that all the stories were fictional. Several times that evening, others asked the same question. "Was that a true story?" and I answered the same way. Finally one woman said, "I just can't get over it. You keep telling us these are fictional stories, but I get taken in every time. I keep thinking these are true stories." People tend to believe what they see instead of what they hear.

My gestures, facial expressions, and body movements told the audience I was talking about literal events. In the opposite way, some speakers tell their audience that what they are saying is true, but they don't know that their body is conveying, "I'm not telling the truth." GESTURES Moving our hands and arms is natural to most of us, so you need to learn how to use gestures in ways that will enhance your presentation. Having said that, I'll add something you probably don't want to hear: You need to learn to speak with your hands hanging by your side. I can hear you say, "But it doesn't feel natural. It's hard. It makes me feel stupid." During the next church service, look around and see what the hands are doing. They are in pockets, crossed, on hips, or holding a purse, Bible, music, or each other. In our society, it is almost universal that people do not like the feeling of their hands hanging by their sides. It feels even more awkward when a person stands up in front of people. If they don't have a podium to hold, they will end up gesturing endlessly. I know it feels awkward, but you need to learn to stand in front of people and talk with your hands by your side. Then when you gesture, move your hands up and out to the front. When the gesture is done, the hands go back down to the side. Here are a few exercises that will help. While you are alone, tell a story without using your hands at all. No, it doesn't count if you put them in your pocket. Throughout the entire story, allow them to hang by your side. Once you have done this, ask someone to listen to you tell a story with your hands by your side. This will break the habit of nervous hands and will help draw the emphasis to your face. Okay, so you don't like that exercise. Here is another activity that is a bit easier. Whenever you are standing in a group meeting (like a church service), allow your hands to hang by your side. No one is looking at you, so they don't know what your hands are doing. It is a simple exercise, but it is effective in helping you with this problem. Of course, gesturing is part of our normal body movement, so here are a few guidelines for making it work for you. Rarely is it appropriate to gesture below the waist. It implies something that is shifty and secretive. It also communicates, "I'm scared!" Since this is not what you want to convey, move your hands higher when you gesture. Likewise, gestures above the shoulders usually mean excitement, panic, praise, surprise, or worship. Save big, high gestures for these uses. In all other situations keep your hands below the shoulders. Most gestures, therefore, should be above your waist and below your shoulders. When you distinctly place them there, it denotes confidence and poise. DON'T GIVE NERVOUSNESS THE FREEDOM TO GESTURE I watched a missionary use the same hand gesture throughout his presentation. We stopped listening to him and started watching his annoying gesture. Some started silently counting how many times he used it during one sermon—96, 97, 98 ... We have all watched children in the preschool department get up and sing their part in a church program. Some wave at parents; others pull their dresses up over their heads; still others stop everything and stare at the audience with their mouths open. They will sway back and forth, twiddle their hair with a finger, call out to parents, cry, twirl their pant legs, or turn to a friend and start talking. We all smile, think it is cute, take pictures, and are thankful we don't have nervous movements anymore. Don't kid yourself. We all have them no matter how experienced we are at public speaking. It might be walking back and forth, curling a mustache, repeating a hand gesture, playing with jewelry, keeping hands in pockets, rocking back and forth, or looking at only one person in the audience. I have some and so do you. It is what makes every speaker different. The key is to recognize they are there and work on them. It is okay to be nervous while you are onstage. In fact, I recommend it. Chapter 11 will teach you to use it to your advantage. For now, know this. Don't give nervousness the freedom to gesture. It never communicates the right message. I often ask a friend if I have an unconscious motion. It is surprising how quickly I get an answer. Others see it and think I already know that I am doing it. But of course I don't. Part of correcting a nervous gesture is finding out we have one. And believe me, we all have them. GIVE IT A TRY: Now, let's get back to the story we are working on together. Stand in front of a mirror and tell "A Girl and Her Dreams," but the only sound you can make is hums. Tell the whole story with facial expressions, body movements ... and hums. IMPERFECTIONS These tips are not meant to discourage you but rather to help. Remember, I stutter every time I get up to speak. Those who hear me have come to expect it. In the same way, your imperfections will distinguish who you are. Throw yourself into your story. Commit your total body to the process. Practice what you have learned, but in the end—be yourself.

16
Talking ; Not Talking

Once I heard Beth Horner tell "The Three Bears," except she did it with a kazoo in her mouth. Instead of words, we heard kazoo humming. We laughed and laughed, because we understood every word. The story relied on facial expressions, gestures, and body movements. Compare telling a story to a painting. There is more on the canvas besides talking. The large brushstrokes are facial expressions and body movements. Words are the small detail brushstrokes. In this chapter we'll focus on control and use of your voice. Tool #4: The Voice Once my father saw me hammering a nail with an adjustable wrench. Instantly he knew it was time for another lecture. I heard it so often. "There is a right tool for every job." I could give the lecture myself, which of course I did when I had children of my own. The voice is a tool we must develop, train, control, carefully use, and never abuse. Here are some ways to properly use this tool. SLOW DOWN As I said in the last chapter, don't allow your voice to dominate the stage. If you talk quickly through a story, you will be robbing time from hand gestures, face, pauses, and body movements. They need their chance to participate. To use the voice to its maximum potential, we must learn to balance it with all the other storytelling tools. Sometimes I choose a story only to realize I don't have enough time to do it justice. To get through it I would have to talk too much. At that point, I have two choices. I could select part of the story and develop that into a full presentation. Or I could set that story aside and simply select a shorter one. CONTROL THE QUALITY As humans, we talk at several different levels of clarity. We can mumble to family members and they will understand what we say. Just because your friends can understand you one-on-one doesn't mean you can be understood in front of a crowd. Record one of your public performances and evaluate how clear your words are. A good exercise is to tell your stories at a retirement home. The residents won't be bashful about telling you how well they can hear and understand you. WORD CHOICE It is never right to be vulgar or obscene. While this is a Christian standard, it is also a standard of professional ethics. Those who violate it reduce the number of people who want to hear them. I tell a story-poem called "The Cremation of Sam McGee," written by Robert Service. The poem has a few words I do not feel comfortable using. They are not appropriate for all audiences. I simply substitute words I can use, and the audience doesn't know the difference. STRAINING YOUR VOICE Your voice is a valuable storytelling tool and key to your success as a communicator. So there is never a good excuse for damaging it. You should protect it like a professional violinist protects her instrument. Your voice is more valuable than any individual story, ball game, joke, argument, or sermon point. Violating this principle is like winning an individual battle by sacrificing the war. I crafted a story in which I needed to make loud noises that portray several frightened animals. The first time I told it, I knew I had strained my voice. Since I liked the story, I knew I had to find a way to tell it without continuing to strain my voice. For a week I practiced those loud noises, trying to see how loud I could make them without straining. I would drive down the street making sounds like a mountain lion, timber wolf, crow, and cattle rustler. At one stoplight, I looked over at the car next to mine and realized the people were looking at me. I smiled, hoping it would assure them of my sanity. Today they would assume I was simply talking on my phone. I may have looked silly, but I was able to perfect the sounds with just enough volume without any strain. I still tell that story today. CHANGING YOUR VOICE The first time I heard Gene Gryniewicz tell a story, I was thrilled and thought, What a great opportunity, to hear a Russian storyteller. I wonder when he immigrated here. Sometime later, I got to hear Gene again, and I was ready to hear another story from the "Motherland." To my surprise, this time he was Irish, fresh off the boat. I couldn't believe it. Later I had a chance to talk with him and found out he was an American from Chicago. Gene works hard at perfecting his accents. Most other storytellers (like me) are not willing to work that hard and usually massacre the accent of another country. Unless you are willing to put the effort into it, you should leave accents alone. Sometimes men use a high falsetto voice when trying to imitate a woman talking. This is usually pitiful and isn't realistic at all. Instead, add a slight change to your voice as you portray different characters, whether it is a woman's or man's voice, old or young, saintly or mean, Irish or Jewish. GIVE IT A TRY: If you have organized a small storytelling group, here is an activity they will enjoy. Assign each person one of the following characters. Have each give his interpretation of how that character would sound. · a cranky old woman: "Get out of my yard!" · a mean troll: "Who's that crossing my bridge?"

· each of the bears: "Someone's been sitting in my chair!" · friendly Irish person: "Top of the morning to you." · a grumpy old man: "Where are my glasses?" · Goliath: "Am I a dog, that you come to me with sticks?" WARMING UP Telling a story is much like singing a song—the voice must be warmed up. I watch people speak before a crowd, and know they haven't warmed up their voices. Words crack, throats are cleared, and before long voices are fading. How much easier it would have been if they had simply gone through a few warm-up exercises. The amount of warm-up time depends on how long a person is going to talk. I won't spend a half an hour to warm up if I am only going to tell a ten-minute story. Instead, I will do some voice exercises for about five or six minutes. When I present one of my six-hour workshops, I will take the time to warm up my voice thoroughly. For simple occasions, the easiest way to warm up is to quietly sing a variety of songs. I usually choose songs that force me to go low and high. In addition, I do the normal "ha, ha, ha, he, he, he, ho, ho, ho, hu, hu, hu" exercises. It is important to start softly and slowly increase the volume. I personally use a technique that helps me sing quietly. I cup my hand near my ear, which amplifies my voice. In this way it doesn't take much volume to hear myself. Treat your voice as a valuable instrument (which it is), and it will help you impact your business, family, ministry, and the world around you in general. Tool #5: The Pause Recently I heard a young pastor preach a sermon. I was astounded he spoke for twenty-five minutes and didn't pause one time! It was a constant barrage of words. Because of this, his message was lost on the audience. It reminded me of old-time radio. At first, people feared dead air space on the radio. They knew some noise had to be coming over the airwaves to let their audience know a program was still on. They assumed talking would be the best noise to use. Jack Benny was an early radio personality who became the master of "the Pause." When he pretended to be walking up a sidewalk toward a house, the audience heard him walking; somehow they knew it would take just that long. When he knocked on the door, he waited and hummed a little tune for the amount of time it took for a person to quit what she was doing and get to the door. He gave up precious talking time but gained the imaginations of his listeners. He took the pause to even greater heights once his show was on television. Skillful communication requires the presenter to stop talking regularly. It takes a certain amount of confidence to stop talking when standing in front of a crowd of people. Learn to reduce your material, reduce your talking, and give more time for silent communication. Here are reasons why "the Pause" is so valuable. IT ENCOURAGES THE PAINTING OF MENTAL PICTURES Buddy was top dog.... [pause—people wonder if the words "top dog" are an expression or a literal dog] When Buddy walked down the street,

[pause] all the other dogs just moved out of the way, [pause] because they knew Buddy was top dog ... [pause—people don't know what the dog looks like, so they will picture him their own way until I give more information.] As I move through the story of Buddy, I continue to give people time to picture everything. I could tell the story in half the time, but the audience would not be able to process it as well. When telling a story, we want our listeners to watch it on their own mental movie devices. They need time to transfer what we say into images. Our actions during the brief pauses help fill out what they are envisioning. IT ALLOWS TIME TO EMPHASIZE FACIAL EXPRESSIONS Don't be like Fred, who was telling a story and suddenly remembered he was supposed to be putting in pauses. So he quickly added some here and there, but at the most unusual places. He would abruptly stop talking with no expression on his face. Here is an important way to learn how to pause naturally. Watch people talk one-on-one. A transcript of their conversation wouldn't make sense. That is because huge chunks of dialogue are dedicated to the rolling of eyes, mischievous winks, raised eyebrows, narrowing mouths, wrinkles in a forehead, hand movements, gentle shoves, little laughs, and so on. IT CREATES ANTICIPATION When I tell stories at libraries, I see mothers bringing their children in to the room. Their plan is to wait until the first story starts, then slip away to browse the shelves and have some time alone. I start the first story, filling it with anticipation pauses. Mom sidles to the back of the room. As I continue to weave the story, the room becomes quiet. The eyes of every child start to widen. Mom is still there, listening. I slowly sway; my hands frame mental pictures; my face takes on the look of each character; and the story intensifies. Deep silence moves across the room. Mom finds a seat. She stays until she and the kids go home together. Anticipation pauses are most effective if they come in the middle of the sentence rather than at the end. For example, in "Saul of Tarsus," I say, "I'm not your usual everyday Jew. Oh, no, I am ... a Pharisee. And not just your everyday, run-of-the-mill Pharisee. Nooooo ... you see ... I ... am a member of ... the Sanhedrin." IT GIVES LIFE TO THE CHARACTERS People often say, "Some storytellers are easy to listen to. It's like they're simply talking to you." There is magic, beauty, and power in storytelling. By slowing down, pausing, adding face and body to the story, you stimulate imagination and bring life to the characters. Even reluctant listeners are drawn in. They are forced to put aside their thoughts until you are finished. If your story is mostly words with very few pauses, people have to work hard to concentrate. It's not easy. They have to keep their focus on your words. Eventually, it becomes too hard and their minds leave you and go into their own imaginations. That is when they become restless. A story with good pauses gives everyone time to get lost in the

story and grow silent. Within that deep silence, the characters have life. The focus is no longer on you. IT DECREASES THE USE OF FILLER WORDS When you are compelled to fill every moment with sound, you will find yourself saying, "uh," "well," "so," "kinda," "you know," "you see," "ha, ha," "sorta," or "anyway." Slowing down helps storytellers think about the mood of the story, while carefully placing each character in the proper spot. We don't think about having to eliminate fillers; we simply no longer have room for them. GIVE IT A TRY: Now, let's get back to the story we are working on together. Get along and slowly tell "A Girl and Her Dreams" and pause as often as you can. Tell it more slowly than you would ever tell it publicly. This will seem strange, but it will bring you new freedom as you learn to create moods and paint mental pictures.

17

Turing Your Weakness Into Strength

*If you are nervous about public speaking, I trust this chapter will change your attitude about getting on stage. You may wonder how I can stand in front of thousands of people and openly stutter. Believe me, I am the poster child for those who get nervous in front of people. This chapter is for people like me. The first step is to realize nervousness is not a weakness at all. It is a platform tool that produces great benefits. Tool #6: Nervousness "Are you nervous tonight, John?" Jan noticed I was quiet as we drove to my speaking event. "Yes, I'm nervous, and it's great." I consider it great because I know I'll do a better job once I feel my nervousness. We should not hate being nervous. When I don't feel it, then I really start to get nervous. As I wait to go on stage, my stomach tightens; a flutter moves through my body; my breath gets short and my palms sweat. My thinking goes like this. Why do I do this to myself? I don't need this. Others look so calm when they get in front of people. It is so natural for them. Obviously, I am not cut out to do this type of thing. When people tell you they never get nervous, it is because they have given it a different name. This is legitimate because they have gained control of it and are using it to their advantage. Be assured, they are as nervous as you, even though they call it something else. Here are several reasons we should value nervousness: * It is a gift. To value nervousness, we must acknowledge it as a gift from God—a gift for us to treasure. The Lord created human bodies and supplied them with exactly what they need to function at their highest potential. Like so many other gifts from God, we overlook its value and only see how it makes us uncomfortable. * It prompts us to prepare. We don't want to fail on stage when everyone is watching. This makes us nervous, which should prompt us to be well prepared. Note this formula: prepare until it is enough, and* *then prepare some more. It's simple, but it works. God's gift works in us to the advantage of our listeners. My stuttering causes me to be more nervous than most people are. Because of it, my preparation is usually more thorough. Rarely do I step on stage without knowing exactly what is going to happen. * It activates our senses. Before you step on stage, fear warns you about what may happen. Fear threatens, "Your mind will go blank! You'll stand with your mouth half open and have nothing to say. Your audience is going to laugh at you." Sweat beads up on your forehead. But don't worry. Nervousness will come to your rescue. As you step on stage, it pours adrenaline into your system. Suddenly your mind is sharp and full of ideas. Your smile becomes crisp and genuine. Optimism takes control. You interact with the audience at your highest ability level. Your talents are sharpened, your senses are awake, and your mind is alert. As you stand in front of an audience, ideas flood your mind that never came as you were sitting in your chair. As you stand in front of people, all your preparation is at your fingertips ready for use. But this adrenaline can also cause you problems. This happens if you craft your story in private and practice giving it in a room by yourself. You can know your material but be unprepared for the heightened senses that come with the adrenaline of facing the audience. That surge of alertness can cause you to go blank if you are not accustomed to it. Practicing your stories in front of people helps you deal with adrenaline in smaller doses. Always rehearse your stories in front of people. * It gives us an extra surge of energy. A nationally known speaker told of a time when he suffered from a bad knee. He was sure the audience felt sorry for him as he hobbled up to the platform. That all changed once he started his speech. He walked effortlessly across the stage; he knelt down as he usually did, and even hopped off the stage and back on. He was having a great time, and his energy was at its highest point. He finished his hour-long talk and stepped down from the platform. Suddenly, all the pain came back into his body, and then some. Most speakers will testify that there were times when they were in no shape to step up on stage. They suffered from headaches, sore muscles, pain, sickness—and yes—stuttering. But as soon as they started their speech or story, all was forgotten until they walked off stage. Nervousness is a gift from God that will help you make your presentation even when you are physically weak. It will help you prepare, make your mind alert, and give you energy. BRINGING NERVOUSNESS UNDER CONTROL A wild horse can do a lot of damage until it is brought under control. Then it becomes a valuable asset. Your nervousness can disable you if you let it run wild. Here are some tips on how to take control of it so it can start benefiting you. * Thank God for it. Once you realize you are nervous, smile, accept it, and thank God for it. By doing this, you are focusing* *your attention on who gave you this nervousness. This causes you to ask, "Why did God give this to me?" Ah, now you are focused on how this great gift is going to help you. It doesn't change how it makes you feel. No, no, you need that! It simply redirects your focus. * Be solid with the platform. Don't let nervousness walk around. Feel the platform beneath you and be solid with it. Feel how comfortable it is to stand there and look around. Walking may be a part of your presentation, so you can choose to walk. Just don't let nervousness make the choice for you. There is another reason to be thinking about the platform. Nervousness wants to move up into your face. If you allow this, you will feel a shortness of breath, and grittiness will settle in around your mouth, nose, and eyes. Push nervousness down. Think about the stage and how solid it feels beneath your feet. * Be conscious of your hands. We've talked about hands, but it's important to reiterate these points. As your hands dangle by your side, you will sense how strange they feel. They are complaining to you. They want to be drawn up, waved around, allowed to hold something, or at least hide in your pockets. Don't give in to them. If you lose this battle, they will be out of control the whole time you are on stage. Hands are not free to do what they want to do. They should concentrate on helping you, not looking out for their own comfort. Soon they will participate in the telling of a story. For now they are helping you by focusing your attention down. It will take all your concentration to keep them under control. * Move emotions to the middle. Move your emotions to your middle by breathing deeply and feeling the breath in the lower part of your abdomen. Consciously move all your feelings down. When you make your first gesture, be conscious of your hands being in front of you. All of these things draw your attention down away from your face. * Draw strength from God's storehouse. Don't fake excitement. False enthusiasm is from the face and not from the depths of the soul. You have the storehouse of God at your disposal. When I know I am not emotionally equipped to stand in front of a crowd, I look to God for help and make a withdrawal from His storehouse. His enthusiasm is real and goes to the depths of the soul. It provides calmness to the spirit and brings nervousness down where I can control it. Tool #7: Confidence Telling a story is not your first job when you step in front of your listeners. There will be plenty of time for that. First, you must pay attention to the business at hand. It is your job to relax the audience. For them to get into your story quickly, they have to know they can trust you. When you step up, they are looking for confidence in your eyes, face, gestures, and mannerisms. They are concerned about your ability to keep their interest, and they need a little reassurance before you get too far into your presentation. There is only one way to put an audience at ease. You must look like you are confident. The audience wants to see you* *have made an emotional investment in your presentation. It starts to put them at ease if it's clear you trust what you are about to do. Think of confidence as the sprinkles atop a cupcake. They don't do much to improve the taste, but they make a person want to give the cupcake a try. Sprinkles won't help if you don't have a good story or don't present it well. But if your product is good, this will make it even better. The following are sprinkles that will entice the listeners to give your story a try. From there, it is up to you to make it good. CONFESSIONS ARE RARELY APPROPRIATE An apology before a performance is an unrefined way of asking for reassurance. An apology after a performance is a crude way of asking for a compliment. Neither is appropriate, and both are unprofessional. · If your preparation is not adequate, the audience doesn't need to hear about it in advance. They will find out soon enough. · It is not the listeners' problem if your abilities are not as good as someone else's. They came to hear your presentation. Get on with it, and let them judge who's better. · Simply standing up and starting to tell the story will cover a lot of deficiencies. Save your apologies for when you have personally offended someone. PRACTICE USING THE MICROPHONE Some start their presentation by telling the audience their opinions about the microphone. Others put the microphone aside because they are not comfortable with it. This causes the audience to groan inwardly. Neither of these actions portrays confidence to the audience. Professional speakers value this modern-day wonder and learn to be comfortable with it. You are only one hour away from being comfortable with microphones for the rest of your life. Go to the person in charge of the amplification system at a church. Ask if you can practice using their system when no one else is in the auditorium. Once you are there, do every crazy thing you can think of with the microphone. Tell stories, make strange sounds, and practice different voices. Talk straight into it, and compare that to having the microphone slightly to the side. Decide whether you like the microphone in your hand or if you prefer having it on a stand. Compare both of these to a lapel mic. One hour of this and you are set for the rest of your life. SOUND CHECK When you are asked to make a presentation, find out in advance if you will need a microphone. If you do, go to the location at least thirty minutes in advance of the presentation. No matter who is in the audience at that time, test out the system to eliminate any surprises before you stand before the crowd. PUTTING IT ALL INTO PRACTICE Ethel Barrett, who wrote the classic Storytelling, It's Easy, talks about who is to have center stage. This quote from her will help put everything into perspective. A story, if it is to fulfill its purpose, ruthlessly demands the center of the stage, so its characters can come to life and have their being. You as a storyteller must make a choice. This, if you have followed all instructions, is not going to be easy to take. Now that you have practiced all the ways and means and know all the tricks—most of them you must forget. At least you must forget them as such. And in time, you will. They will become a part of you, and you will not be conscious of them as techniques—they are just you, but a newly developed and disciplined you, lifted to a higher plane of artistry. And the day will finally come when you realize that there is not room on the platform for both you and the story; one of you has to go. That will be the day when you forget yourself completely, lose your identity in the story. You are the story. It is the highest form of art.*

18
Why Storytelling

I'd like you to go on this trip with me." As I said this to Jan, I knew there were limits on how often I could say it. She doesn't like to travel, but we have a standing agreement. She will go with me on any trip as long as I tell her it is important to me. So as soon as the words left my mouth, she stopped, turned, and looked at me. It was now time for me to quickly give my reasons. "Somehow I think what I learn on this trip will greatly influence the rest of our lives. I want you there to hear it firsthand." We packed the car and headed for Fort Worth, Texas. It was January 2003, the same month Moody Publishers first released The Art of Storytelling. But I wasn't going to Texas to conduct training in storytelling; I was going to receive training in storytelling. CHRONOLOGICAL BIBLE STORYING I have taught thousands of people how to embellish Bible stories so they can put their lessons inside their telling of a story. I have also trained people on how to increase their personal storytelling skills. But this was different. J.O. Terry and Grant Lovejoy were conducting a seminar on Chronological Bible Storying. They were teaching a concept that was totally new to me. We were being taught how to craft and tell Bible stories that were completely accurate to Scripture, with nothing added to "spice it up." In fact, our instructors said a person doesn't have to be good at telling stories to be successful at this. We soon found that almost everyone else in attendance at this training was a missionary to a foreign country. They were there to learn this new approach, chronological storying, used by missionaries around the world. HOW WE LEARN During this training was the first time I heard that 75 percent of the Bible is written in a story format. They said God had it written this way to make it easier for people to learn, remember, and share with others. When I asked about the other 25 percent, I was surprised to learn that 15 percent of the Bible is in some form of poetry, and only 10 percent is in analytical reasoning. That week of training changed our direction in life.

I went home and started to experiment with "storying." Soon I became friends with Dr. Mark Getz, a rheumatologist who lives about an hour's drive from us. He had been interested in chronological storying for several years. He said, "Would you like to experiment using this with my adult Sunday school class?" This started a fifteen-week venture. I traveled to his church each Sunday and taught thirty-five adults to tell a Bible story, a different one each week. After ten weeks, I asked the participants, "Why do you keep coming to this class week after week?" One man said, "John, you are teaching us stories our pastor assumes we already know." After the fifteen weeks, I continued crafting the stories, and Mark taught the class until they had learned to tell seventy-two stories— thirty-six from the Old Testament and thirty-six from the life of Christ. I tried teaching the process to other churches in the United States, but they found it totally different from anything they knew. To them, Bible stories are for children. They were sure that adults need "solid" teaching. OPENING DOORS Immediately, doors started opening in other countries. Missionaries and national Christian leaders were eager to learn more about BibleTelling, and how it would help them reach and teach the people in their countries. Unlike people in American churches, they were eager to get this new tool. Still, I knew my mission field was the U.S., where storying was not yet being accepted. God used this time to teach me more about storying, and how it can be used in ministry. J.O. Terry reassured me that eventually American churches would wake up to this tremendous tool. He was right. Now I see churches changing. Pastors have been hearing about what is happening on the mission field. They suddenly realize how little of the Word of God their people really know. Their people know doctrine, theology, Christian ethics, and proper relationships—what they don't know are the stories of the Bible. Church leaders are coming to the realization that preaching, based on sound reasoning, helps people form good doctrine. Knowing the stories of the Bible helps us make good decisions. Our churches are in a state of crisis because the people know doctrine but don't know the stories behind it. Churches are full of people with good doctrine who are not transferring what they know to making wise decisions! POOL OF TRUE STORIES We make all decisions based on the stories in our lives that we think are true. I call this our "pool of true stories." It forms our worldview. These come from all the stories in our lives—family happenings, history of our nation, folktales, fairy tales, gossip, and everyday events. We gain more "true stories" by what we watch on television, hear from friends, read in books, and learn from the office. People from every nation and culture justify what they do based on what is in their pool of true stories. Even gang members are convinced their actions are sound because they match up with *their experience of true stories. God created us to have this pool and then gave us the Bible, which is made up of true stories. He says, "If you hide My word (my stories) in your heart, it will keep you from sin (bad decisions)." ALL THE STORIES OF THE BIBLE Every Christian should get a daily dose of Bible stories, in addition to their other spiritual studies. To make it easy, I have crafted Bible stories that cover all the events of the Bible. Each story is accurate to Scripture, with nothing added to embellish what is given in the Bible. It is the "simple telling" of a biblical event. Everything has been removed that distracts from the simple understanding of the story. Also nothing in the story is left out because of offensive content. In other words, it is not specifically written for children. I blend several smaller stories together to make up one larger story. If an event appears more than once in the Bible, I compile the accounts into one story called All the Stories of the Bible. These are available as a free download (pdf) at www.BibleTelling.org. All of this makes it easy to read and understand the flow of Scripture. "I UNDERSTAND THE BIBLE!" One person said she never read the Bible because she couldn't understand it. She didn't even own a copy. I challenged her to read All the Stories of the Bible. She was reluctant at first but finally started reading it. She knew I simplified the stories, so she was curious about what I left out of each one. So she looked up each story in the Bible. She said, "I found if I read the story first and then read it in the Bible, I understand the Bible! Your book doesn't replace the Bible; it is a portal to the Bible!" USING BIBLE STORIES Missionaries have been using BibleTelling and other storying materials for years. We are constantly experimenting with exciting ways to use these stories. Here are some reasons why you'll want to enhance your ability at BibleTelling. * Reading vs. Telling You can use Bible stories in a family and ministry situation without having to tell them by memory. They are crafted in a conversational format, so they can easily be read to others. The difference between reading and telling is in the person giving the story. There is a tremendous spiritual advantage in learning to tell the stories of Scripture. It has an impact on one's life like few other activities. This is the reason Christians around the world have taken a new interest in learning Bible stories. They have been surprised how it affects their spiritual life and their ability to make right decisions. Most have noticed this after learning only ten stories. * Hiding God's Word in Your Heart "Hiding God's Word in your heart" is more than memorizing verses from the Bible—although that is important. Learning to tell the stories of the Bible is one way a person can easily learn Scripture and remember it for life. In the next chapter I'll give you some easy steps on how to learn and remember stories without just memorizing words. * Equipping for Ministry There is another great advantage in learning*

Bible stories. It is the key for helping laypeople get involved in ministry. It takes years to become good at preaching. It takes unique skills to be a musician or part of a drama team. But with just a little effort, anyone can learn to tell stories and use them in ministry. Now that you're motivated, read on; the next chapter will help you get started learning Bible stories.

19

THE STORYTELLER

God created people to tell and listen to stories. When given truth, they can understand it quickly if they hear it within a story, poem, or song. Even so, Bible teachers are trained to only use analytical logic when explaining Scripture. Missionaries are now teaching national pastors how to tell Bible stories, so they can better relate to the people within their community. Of course these pastors are also trained to become skillful at analyzing the Bible and presenting a logical argument for the truths of Scripture. There needs to be a balance of both skills. STORY SELECTION In the past I felt it important to carefully select which Bible stories I use with those who haven't yet accepted the Christian message. This type of story set is often referred to as going "from Creation to Christ." I still believe in doing this. Recently, several of my nonbelieving friends selected their own Bible stories to read and learn. To my chagrin, I found they had chosen some of the strangest stories in the Bible! Then I was amazed to see how those stories totally impacted their lives for Christ. Three lines of the triangle 1. LINE BETWEEN THE STORYTELLER AND THE LISTENER —There is a natural tendency to listen to a story. Requirement: Be willing to tell a story poorly. A few years ago, I was in the children's section of my local library looking for a story for a program. In the corner of the room was the typical scene of a librarian reading a book to a group of wide-eyed children. They sat on the floor around her not saying a word, totally lost in their imagination. Behind the children were several rows of bookshelves. A man was standing in the first row, so there was only one shelf of books between him and the librarian reading the story. Obviously the story had grabbed him. His body was standing there, but his mind was with those children in the world of imagination. He suddenly realized what he was doing. He became embarrassed at being hooked by a story crafted for preschoolers. He quickly looked around to see if anyone was watching him. And of course, there was— me. To break the grip of that story, he had to move from that row and get far enough away so he couldn't hear her. People who don't want to listen to a story have to fight the urge when one is being told. Some people put up a wall of resistance when they know a story is coming their way. I have learned how to get around that wall. The key is not to warn them you are about to tell a story. Try not to say "That reminds me of a story" or "Let me tell you a story" or "That reminds me of a time when ..." If you simply start the story, people will listen to it. —Telling a Story Poorly Two facts equal a sad truth. Fact #1: All of us tell a story poorly the first few times we tell it. Fact #2: We are to practice our stories in front of people. The sad truth = We have to go through the "poorly" stage in front of people. It all comes down to this. If you aren't willing to tell stories poorly, you won't tell them at all. Therefore, the fear of telling a story poorly has kept many people from telling Bible stories. This is the big difference between people who have a natural ability to tell stories and those who don't. The first group is willing to stumble through a story and tell it poorly a time or two. —The 5-Time Rule The 5-time rule is the secret of success in BibleTelling and storytelling in general. A story doesn't become good until the teller has told it five times to other people. · The first telling of a story is awful, but that's the way it is. You start it wrong, stumble through the middle, forget part of it, and then leave it hanging at the end. No wonder people avoid telling stories! But—when you first tell a story, it's important to forget part of it. You'll never forget that part again because it is burned into your memory! · On to the second telling of the story. Things have greatly improved. You have figured out a better way to start it. You remember the parts you forgot the last time, but you forget other parts (good for you). The ending still isn't smooth, but much better. Now you are starting to notice how people are reacting to the story. It is becoming clear what parts of the story keep their interest and what parts cause their minds to wander. · The third time, the story starts to take shape. The biggest problem is that you are still thinking about the words of the story. · By the fourth telling, it's beginning to flow out of you. · When you tell it the fifth time, you aren't thinking about how you are doing it. You will see that the story definitely draws in your listeners. Now you have a story you can tell for the rest of your life. After the fifth telling, people will start saying you have a natural gift for storytelling. 2. LINE BETWEEN THE STORYTELLER AND THE BIBLE STORY —an easy and natural way to communicate Requirement: Learn to tell stories without memorizing words. Imagine I see a good friend after a church service. I say, "Steve, how did that fishing trip go?" "Hi John. Hey, it was great! As soon as I got there, I ..." I may have listened to a great sermon that was the result of education, training, experience, study, and preparation—but there's a good chance I won't remember it the next day. In contrast, Steve has my total attention as he tells me about his fishing trip, and for the next week I'll remember exactly what he said. Steve is not a professional storyteller. He isn't telling this story because of his educational background. He isn't using notes to make sure he gets it straight. He hasn't memorized his lines, and he isn't worried about forgetting something. No, he is simply telling me about an event. If he did forget something, I'm sure the next time I see him, he'll say, "Oh John. I forgot to tell you ..." Herein is the key to the relationship between the storyteller and the story. Learn to tell a Bible story without memorizing words. You should tell it as naturally as Steve told me about his fishing trip. Example of Conversational Storytelling A guy at work says to you, "Say, you go to church. Maybe you can clear something up for me. I heard someone talking about the Bible the other day. He said something about a man who wanted to find a wife for his son, so he sent a servant to go get one. I don't know. Maybe I'm getting it all wrong. Do you know of a story like that?" Well, it happens that you were reading All the Stories of the Bible. The day before you had read "Rebekah." So you say, "Sure, I know that story. I was just reading it the other day. "How does it go?" In that situation, you wouldn't rush home and memorize every word in the story. You wouldn't set up a stage at the workplace with microphones and lights. You wouldn't dress up in costume and perform the story. Not at all. You would simply tell him the story in about two minutes, hitting the highlights as you remembered them. That is conversational storytelling, and that is how most Bible stories are told. Storyboards—tools for remembering the essential parts of a story Your road to learning Bible stories starts with developing the ability to "see the story" and tell others what you see. We call this developing a "storyboard" in your mind. People use many different types of storyboards according to their personality and preference. The following steps will help you find a storyboard that fits you best. If possible, find another person to work with you. Actually it is best if four people work together on this. Each should have a different Bible story. Select stories from All the Stories of the Bible found on BibleTelling.org. 1. If you have four people, number off 1, 2, 3, 4. Now subdivide with 1 and 2 being partners and 3 and 4 being partners 2. Each of you silently read your own story twice. 3. Summarize the story to your partner in two or three sentences. 4. Take a pencil and divide the story into scenes. Usually there are three to five scenes per story. 5. Go through each scene, underlining people and important things. 6. In 3 minutes, roughly sketch each scene on paper. (Do NOT draw well. This should be done quickly. Most people use stick figures.) 7. Add cartoon-like speech bubbles to represent the spoken words or thoughts within the story. Do NOT add the words. 8. Explain your picture to your partner, but don't tell the story at this point. 9. You and your partner walk around separately and place various people and activities of the story in different parts of the room. 10. Take your partner to each spot in the room and explain what part of the story is there. Don't tell the story at this point, simply describe where everything is located, especially where the conversation bubbles occur. 11. Walk around the room by yourself and read the story aloud—looking at where you have placed each part. 12. Put away your paper copy of the story. 13. Select another partner from your group of four and tell him/her the story as you walk around the room. 14. Tell the story to the last person in your group, but don't walk around the room as you tell it. 15. Tell your story a total of five times within the next week. 3. LINE BETWEEN THE BIBLE STORY AND THE LISTENER —it is the work of the Holy Spirit to apply the story to the life of the listener Requirement: Learn to trust the power of a Bible story. The triangle has one line that doesn't involve the storyteller. It is the line between the Bible story and the listener. As a BibleTeller, you select the story and control how you tell it. You select the listener and control what story you will tell. But you can't control what effect the story will have on the listener. They learn what the Holy Spirit wants them to learn. The more I go on in life, the more I realize that the Word of God is not dependent on my added comments. —Preaching Pastors often think I am saying they shouldn't apply the story to the lives of the people they serve. That is not what I'm saying. Pastors are called by God and trained to explain the Scripture. Even so, they will admit it is the Holy Spirit who takes their words and applies it to the hearts of the people. It is my purpose to encourage those who are not pastors. You don't need to understand the entire Bible to be used by the Holy Spirit. Learn the stories and tell them. You don't have to explain them. It is amazing what happens when your listeners are allowed to discover for themselves what a Bible story is teaching them. Many times Jesus explained the Scriptures to His disciples. But other times He simply told a story and let the Holy Spirit bring the truth home to His listeners. We need to use both of these approaches.

I thought about this for the rest of the service. I couldn't figure out how this truth (which I had known for years) was so wrong. And yet I knew from experience that it wasn't wrong. Most Christians did accept Christ before the age of twelve. But I also knew that many of the children who did accept Christ dropped out of church during their teenage years. For that next week, I went on a search. I kept asking, "What happens at age twelve?" I talked to people who worked with children and people who worked with teenagers. Finally I found it. It stuck out like a sore thumb. People were saying, "We stop telling Bible stories at age twelve. We go into the deeper things of God's Word. We talk about doctrine, relationships, Christian ethics, and so on. It is important we not treat teenagers like children." It all made perfect sense, except it doesn't work! People stop putting their faith in Christ, and those who had accepted Him stop coming. All this time we thought people changed at age twelve. We thought they became less receptive to the gospel. How could we ignore the fact that this idea is not found anywhere in the Bible? LOOKING FOR A METHOD This started my efforts at creating an adult Bible class that got back to Bible stories. I felt the class needed to focus on how the stories related to their everyday experiences instead of deep theological teaching. I decided to call this class Experiencing BibleTelling. Dr. Mark Getz and I worked on this concept in many different ways. People in our two churches became frustrated with each of us, but we couldn't stop until we figured it out. LISTENERS, LEARNERS, WORKERS We discovered adults in church fall into one of three groups. · Listeners · Learners · Workers (Oh, don't you wish I had said "Laborers"?) The listeners want to come to a service and just listen. They don't want to be forced into participating. Sometimes I go to church as a listener. I have been in meetings all week. I just want to relax and enjoy someone else doing the talking. I understand listeners, so we had to develop Experiencing BibleTelling so it would appeal to listeners. The learners sign up for a particular Bible study with pen in hand. They sit near the front and take notes. We all love learners. They speak up when asked questions and help in any way they can. Eventually another study strikes their interest and off they go. We had to design Experiencing BibleTelling so it would keep learners interested. The workers look for training that builds their ministry skills. They don't attend too many Bible studies because they are conducting them— or working in another ministry. Once they are convinced about the value of Bible stories, they will learn them on a regular basis. We felt workers didn't need Experiencing BibleTelling. All they needed was this book! Oh, but we were wrong. SUCCESS, BUT NOT SURE We finally came up with a plan. It worked with a couple of groups, but we weren't sure if it would have a wide appeal. So for the next few years, I took it with me as I traveled around the world. A group in Taiwan asked me to be their keynote speaker at their annual five-day summer missionary conference. I told them I wanted to use this new method we developed. To my amazement, they said yes. What a wonderful week it was as I helped them experience the stories of Elijah. Missionaries in Paraguay said it definitely wouldn't work with their people. They set up a special week of meetings so we could see how the people would respond. Again, we had a wonderful week as I helped them experience lesser-known stories of the Old Testament. We have used it with teenagers, pastors, missionaries, prisoners, young professionals, and older ... uh ... people my age. We have seen it work with nationals in Asia, Africa, Europe, and North and South America. A nonbeliever told me, "I might not have dropped out of church if I had been taught the Bible this way." CREATING AN EXPERIENCING BIBLETELLING CLASS After several years of testing the concept, and teaching these principles to others, I asked our pastor if I could start an Experiencing BibleTelling class at our church. We announced it in our morning service, and a few brave souls met on that first Sunday morning during Sunday school time. Our adventure had started. · Three videos are included on the website: "Story of the Week," "Story Insights," and "Minutes with Mickie." We ask the class to watch these videos before coming to class. · Those who watch them do so even if they are going to miss a session. They feel it helps them stay current with the class. · The class starts with someone telling that week's Bible story. · The rest of the time is totally taken up with three activities. 1. Immediately after the story, we ask, "What was your favorite part of that story?" 2. After a few minutes of discussion, we move on to our main activity. Each week, the activity is uniquely designed to fit the story. A sample list is given below. 3. Near the end of class, I ask, "What is the one thing we learn from this story?" This usually prompts several opinions—and a great closing discussion. I can hear you ask, "Is that it? With all of your searching, experimenting, and testing, I thought your program would be highly complicated. This is too simple." It is simple. Still, we constantly have people coming to see it in action. Several of our regular attenders come from other churches. They attend the early service in their church, and then come to our class. BASIC PRINCIPLES FOR USING EXPERIENCING BIBLETELLING 1. No one teaches a lesson. The activities encourage people to share their life experiences with one another. From this, they see how the Bible story relates to present-day life. 2. No one has to participate in any activity. Some people love to come to class, but don't want to say anything—at least at first. Usually they join in as time goes by. 3. It is often better to subdivide the class into smaller groups for activities. Some *people participate easier if they are talking to 4 to 6 people instead of 40 people. 4. Limit the discussion to the story at hand. Experiencing BibleTelling has an appeal to people who know a vast amount of Scripture as well as those who know very little about it. They sit side by side and easily talk about things together. This is possible only because people are asked not to go to other parts of the Bible during our discussions. SAMPLE ACTIVITIES Groups of four to six: · Re-tell the story as a group. · Put parts of the story on cards. Have each group put the cards in chronological order. · Assign several groups to deal with different issues in this story. · How does this story apply to current events, historic events, the pastor's sermon, a book or devotional? · How does [some aspect of this story] remind you of a personal event in your life? · Bumper stickers—summarize what's learned into a bumper sticker. Whole class activities: · Use food to enhance a story. · "Envision the story"—ask "imagination questions" about places and people in the story. People have to answer according to how they saw the story in their mind as it was being told. · "At the Scene"—several members of the class volunteer to answer questions about the biblical event as if they are there covering it for a television news station. · Interviews—key characters from the story (volunteers) are asked to form a panel. The class leader interviews them, asking questions about what happened in the story. People in the class can also ask questions. · Self-evaluation forms. · Three-minute dramas. · Volunteer embellishing an assigned part of the story. · "Clueless"—the class tries to enlighten a volunteer who acts clueless. Clueless keeps asking questions. · Retelling the whole story using the approach of ... Fortunately/Unfortunately, "Oh good/Oh no," "Good news/Bad news." · "Settling out of Court"—people present arguments from various views within story. · Coffee House Discussion—three people discuss events within the story as if they had been there. Another person comes along who had been out of town and missed the whole thing. · Israel map—finding the location of events. · Writing a news story on a biblical event. · This activity is great for a story that has many parts. * Divide the class into as many groups as there are parts in the story. * Give each group a copy of their section of the story (before the telling). * Tell them, "After the story, you are to do two things: 1. Give your section a title. 2. Make a stick figure drawing that illustrates your section of the story. * After each group reports, put their drawing on the wall. · As you tell the story, move to a different location in the room to distinguish between the scenes in the story. Then have different people retell each section while standing in the location where that part of the story took place. · This activity is great for a story that has many geographical areas. * Tell the story. * Have the class identify various geographical areas in the story. * Ask the class to place those locations* *around the room. * Have volunteers stand at each location. * Evenly divide the class to stand with those volunteers. * Have each group draw stick figures that represent what happened at their location. * Have the class arrange the drawings in chronological order. * Each group identifies what characters were at their location. Assign each character to only one location. * Each group tells the class what one thing can be learned from that character. · Phrase Cards: * Divide the class into groups of 3 or 4. * Tell the story. * Give each group a stack of cards with phrases taken from the story (about 24 phrases). * Have the groups put the cards in chronological order. * Once they have done the best they can, re-tell the story and allow them to correct their order as the story is told. · Freeze Frames: (human snapshot of an event) * Select several scenes from the story and assign each scene to a different group. * Give the group several minutes to organize the "freeze frame" that represents their section of the story. * As each group assembles in the front of the room, have everyone else cover their eyes until the performers are ready. * Then everyone opens their eyes and tries to guess what event is being portrayed. · Giving Advice or Words of Wisdom: * Identify the main characters in the story. * Assign one character to each group in the class. * Members of the group discuss how they could advise their character to modify their behavior. It has been amazing to see how Experiencing BibleTelling affects individuals. Many have said it has opened up Scripture in ways they have never seen before. Several have said they didn't learn this much Bible in the seminary they attended. I would say everyone has grown in their walk with God. We are now finding Experiencing BibleTelling is not just for adults. We are having great success using it with all age levels. PUTTING IT INTO PRACTICE Mickie O'Donnell is the author of Workshop Wonders, and president of Lord and King Associates and director of children and family ministries at Noroton Presbyterian church in Darien, Connecticut. Her comments will help put everything into perspective. A few years ago I had 35 fifth graders in an after-school program. Sitting in a large circle I told them the story of Samuel. It started with Hannah's prayer and ended with Eli's death. Once I finished the story, I asked the children to re-tell it, one phrase at a time as we went around the circle. With very few hesitations they re-told the entire story. I then divided them into groups of three and had them re-tell the story to each other as best they could. Once enough time had passed for that experience, the students returned to the big circle and I asked them one question. "What does this story tell you about God?" Immediately hands shot up, eager to share their thoughts. Here are four things these students said: 1. You don't have to be old to hear God's voice. 2. You don't have to be an adult to serve God. 3. If you listen, God will talk to you. 4. When God says He's going to do something, He does it! I sat there amazed!*

If I had used other teaching methodologies, I would have created three points, and backed them up with didactic teaching. My points probably would have been similar to theirs. I'm just not sure they would have listened carefully. However, with BibleTelling, the points of the story came from the listeners themselves, as it moved their hearts and minds. They were much more excited telling me what the story taught. Personally I probably would not have thought of point #4, but God wanted these children to know that point. Since that day, I have continuously had similar experiences in my teaching with children, youth, and adults. Believing that Hebrews 4:12 is true, I have come to fully appreciate the power of the biblical narrative and want to let the Word of God speak. The techniques I have learned and used from storytelling have transformed not only my ministry but me as well. So, there you have it! I hope you've enjoyed our journey through the exciting world of storytelling and BibleTelling. Remember the promise I gave you at the beginning. I said, "If you carefully go through this book and do most of the activities, it will greatly change your ability to tell stories for the rest of your life. It will also enhance your enjoyment, effectiveness, ministry, and the pleasure of those around you." I am confident you have found this to be true. Now, it is time to take the second step. Teach this book to someone else. It will help that person, but it will also take your skills to a much higher level, and totally change your life. You have too much to offer to allow the attention of your audience to wander from what you are saying.

We need to learn how to tell stories, but we should also know why we tell them. Is it possible to tell a good story with our lives? Why do we tell stories at all? The following is an excerpt of Scott McClellan's Tell Me a Story to answer some of those questions.